The Ads That Won The War

Derek Nelson

Motorbooks International
Publishers & Wholesalers ®

First published in 1992 by Motorbooks International
Publishers & Wholesalers, PO Box 2, 729 Prospect Avenue,
Osceola, WI 54020 USA

Motorbooks International is a certified trademark,
registered with the United States Patent Office

The information in this book is true and complete to the
best of our knowledge. All recommendations are made
without any guarantee on the part of the author or
Publisher, who also disclaim any liability incurred in
connection with the use of this data or specific details

We recognize that some words, model names and
designations, for example, mentioned herein are the
property of the trademark holder. We use them for
identification purposes only. This is not an official
publication

Motorbooks International books are also available at
discounts in bulk quantity for industrial or sales-
promotional use. For details write to Special Sales Manager
at the Publisher's address

Library of Congress Cataloging-in-Publication Data
Nelson, Derek.
    The ads that won the war / Derek Nelson.
        p.   cm.
    Includes index.
    ISBN 0-87938-591-X
    1. World War, 1939–1945—Propaganda—Pictorial
works.   2. Propaganda, American—Pictorial
works.   I. Title.
D810.P7U44 1992
940.54′88673—dc20   91–41278

Printed and bound in Hong Kong

On the front cover: *Coca-Cola was one of many companies that
continued issuing colorful, creative ads even though their product
was scarce on the homefront because of strict rationing. Courtesy,
The Coca-Cola Co.*

On the back cover: *Top, this 1943 Allison advertisement features
a Flying Tiger P-40 and a cablegram from Col. Claire Chennault,
leader of the Flying Tigers, thanking the Allison workers for
building reliable engines for their P-40s (Courtesy, General
Motors Corp.). Lower left, this Bell Aircraft ad touts Bell's role in
building machine-gun mounts (Courtesy, Bell Aerospace Textron).
Lower right, a 1942 North American Aviation ad that features
caricatures of Hilter, Mussolini and Tojo. Note the title "Honorary
Aryan" on Tojo's collar (Courtesy Rockwell International Corp.).*

Contents

Jack of all Raids

Target of opportunity, the long suit of any B-25 Mitchell, and when the target does not readily present itself, you can depend on American pilots to make the opportunity. Whether it's a bombing mission requiring pinpoint precision or busting up a jungle troop concentration with lawnmower efficiency, the B-25 takes them all in stride. To the Japs, this rugged plane is nicknamed The Flying Pillbox; to American pilots, it's the work horse of the Army Air Forces.

THREE MODELS OF THE B-25 MITCHELL—EACH DESIGNED FOR A SPECIAL TYPE OF COMBAT OPERATION

PINPOINT

This is the bomb-sight nose of a B-25 Mitchell. This model is used for pinpoint precision bombing from medium altitudes.

PENETRATION

B-25 Mitchell with eight 50-caliber machine guns in the nose. This model used for penetrating jungle undergrowth.

PUNCH

Famed 75 mm cannon nose of the B-25 Mitchell delivers knockouts to pillboxes, punches holes in Jap communications.

North American Aviation *Sets the Pace*

PLANES THAT MAKE HEADLINES...*the P-51 Mustang fighter (A-36 fighter-bomber), B-25 and PBJ Mitchell bomber, the AT-6 and SNJ Texan combat trainer. North American Aviation, Inc. Member, Aircraft War Production Council, Inc.*

Acknowledgments

Some company archives in America are well-established operations, staffed by curators, research specialists, and librarians. Other companies have no records. I encountered both ends of the spectrum while researching this book.

A number of historic companies carefully preserve their traditions. The Coca-Cola Company recently opened a new museum in Atlanta, displaying a wealth of World War II material, including artifacts such as a Coke bottle that was used as an insulator in front-line communications networks. I was lucky to discover that the staff at Oldsmobile's History Center had just finished the chapter about World War II in their in-progress history of the company, and were willing to share their excellent research with me.

In all cases, a company's roots are a matter of interest and pride to current employees, but the documentation is sometimes lost. On the other hand, some company histories appear in books, although many are out of print, particularly those published just after the war. Sometimes, a company's history has never been written, or corporate mergers have broken the lineage of a famous name, leaving the records scattered and lost. Some of the people I talked to and corresponded with around the country invited me to visit and rummage through their filing cabinets. Many others were happy to supply whatever material they had at hand; some members of the postwar generation shared my enthusiasm at discovering the themes and events of the early 1940s.

Assembling this book would have been impossible without the help of scores of people. A handful went above and beyond the normal call of public affairs and corporate relations. At the Oldsmobile Division of General Motors Corporation, Director of Public Rela-

Even though North American had orders for more aircraft than they could possibly build, they never stopped advertising their war-winning fighters, bombers, and trainers. Courtesy, Rockwell International Corp.

tions Gus Buenz, and Helen Jones Earley and Jim Walkinshaw of the Oldsmobile History Center provided in-depth research materials and outstanding photos of the company's conversion to wartime production. At NW Ayer, Incorporated, archives assistants Helen Kim and Lynna Moy, and Legal Department staff member Ann Stone produced a gold mine of company newsletters and ad reproductions and expedited permissions. At Kraft General Foods, Incorporated, Archives Manager Elizabeth Adkins, and archives technicians Steve Carvell and Alissa Berman, put together such a large, interesting, and vivid package that it seemed to demand an entire book of its own.

Dave Gosler, manager for public affairs (Groups and Regions) at General Motors Corporation, kindly gave permission to reproduce a wealth of material from GM's massive trove; any retelling of the story of democracy's arsenal would be woefully incomplete without it. Sharon Schiller, senior trademark counsel White Consolidated Industries, Incorporated, similarly gave me access to the outstanding Nash-Kelvinator series. Nancy Henry and Rose Fronczak of Armstrong World Industries, Incorporated; Joyce Luster, corporate archivist for Caterpillar, Incorporated; and Lois Lovisolo, corporate historian for Grumman Corporation all exhumed and provided hard-to-find advertisements and background materials. At the Maytag Company, Advertising Director Norman W. Boyle and Manager of Marketing and Media Relations Linda Eggerss were helpful, enthusiastic, and the first to respond to my coast-to-coast barrage of inquiries and requests.

Many other people provided documents, photocopies, and recollections that would have been nearly impossible to otherwise obtain. They saved me countless hours in library research and helped make this book more authentic and complete: Daniel Dolan, senior administrator of media relations, and Jack Burks of the Public Affairs and Communications Department, AC Rochester Division, General Motors Corporation; Daniel Lang, vice president of information and public affairs, Association of American Railroads; Alphonso

5

Salandra, director of communications, Bell Aerospace Textron; Larry Gustin of the Public Relations Department, Buick Motor Division, General Motors Corporation; George O. Braatz, public relations manager, Champion Spark Plug Company; Bruce Thomas of the Chrysler Historical Collection; Phil Mooney, manager of the Archives Department, The Coca-Cola Company; Harwood Ritter, manager of corporate marketing communications, Ethyl Corporation; Kristin Chadwell, general counsel, and Amy Stidham of the Department of Citrus, State of Florida; Robert Slayman, publicity director, and Scott Hallman, news and information director, Lockheed Corporation; Elliott Miller, director of public relations, Martin Marietta Corporation; Thomas Ross, vice president of advertising and corporate communications, Oneida Limited; Edward S. Lechtzin, director of public relations, Pontiac Division, General Motors Corporation; John Daggett, director of corporate communications, and Thomas H. Garver, corporate archivist, Rayovac Corporation.

My gratitude also to the following people, listed not by the magnitude of their assistance but alphabetically by company: Miriam Trangsrud Welty, director of public affairs, and Cindy Strowig, manager of corporate records, Abbott Laboratories; Jack Hawks, director of public information, and Laura Kauffman, manager of advertising services, American Gas Association; Marcy Goldstein, archives records manager, and Sheldon Hochheiser, senior research associate, AT&T Bell Laboratories; Ela Wilmanowicz, public relations representative, BorgWarner Automotive Inc.; James Baughman, corporate counsel, and Ralph Collier, president of Campbell Museum, Campbell Soup Company; Christopher A. Taravella, assistant general counsel and chief patent counsel, and J. B. Kuhnie, national advertising manager, Dodge Cars and Trucks, Chrysler Corporation; Randy N. Bergman, communications specialist, Colgate-Palmolive Company; Frances J. Sullivan, senior editor, identity and nomenclature, corporate advertising, Eastman Kodak Company; Alice Schnapier, division vice president of advertising, Fieldcrest Cannon Incorporated; Tom Foote, manager of the Corporate News Department, Ford Motor Company; Ruth Shoemaker, Hall of History Foundation, and Carla M. Fischer, public relations representative, General Electric Company; Beverly Pierce, manager of public relations, The BFGoodrich Company; Mary Manley, senior community relations representative, Goodyear Tire & Rubber Company; Teresa Miller, director of corporate relations, and David Saacke, Genesco Incorporated; Ralph Borland, vice president for marketing, Greyhound Lines, Incorporated; Eileen Guernsey, manager of consumer affairs, Dixie Products Business Division, James River Corporation; D. M. Dickey, senior communications coordinator, Kellogg Company; Sheryl Smith, public relations coordinator, Lever Brothers Company; Mary Bell, consumer relations supervisor, Liggett Group, Incorpo-

rated; Walter Fitzgerald, vice president of marketing, John Middleton Incorporated; Judith A. Moncrieff, manager of public affairs, Mobil Corporation; Sharon S. Darling, director, and Eric Schuster, staff researcher, Motorola Museum of Electronics, Motorola Incorporated; Henry Sandbach, vice president of public relations, and Dave Stivers, Nabisco Brands, Incorporated; John R. Falk, public relations manager, Winchester Group, Olin Corporation; Jo F. Spach, manager of public information, R. J. Reynolds Tobacco Company; June W. Deyerle, Chap Stick brand manager, Consumer Products Division, A. H. Robins Company; Mike Mathews, director of public relations, North American Aircraft, Rockwell International Corporation; Bruce R. Kleinman, manager of publications, Shell Oil Company; Robert Thompson, vice president of public affairs, Springs Industries Incorporated; Tom Bengel, vice president and general manager, Paul Guilden, and Peter Wiederhorn, John B. Stetson Company; W. Michael Keenan, manager, advertising and sales promotion, Texaco Incorporated; Fred Kelley, corporate manager, advertising and promotion, The Boeing Company; Thomas Furlong, public relations specialist, Warner-Lambert Company.

Thanks also to David Pfeiffer of the Washington National Records Center, National Archives, for pointing to the right boxes, and to Thelma Mack of the Reference Department, Portsmouth Public Library, for not setting a deadline on how long I could browse through old magazines in the bowels of the library.

Greg Field, my editor at Motorbooks, was patient and thoughtful, as usual. If he hadn't been able to detect the promise in this unconventional project, this book might not have been written.

My wife Mary viewed and critiqued numerous slide shows of obscure and sometime bizarre ads, listened to me read the text of dozens of others, tolerated my late nights and sporadic absences, and (as she has for the past two decades) kept the faith even when mine wavered. My son Nate deserves a medal for staying excited about yet another book.

Reproduction Permissions

Numerous commercial brand names are mentioned in the text and in the advertisements reproduced in this book. In all cases where the brands mentioned still exist and where the companies that produced the ads still exist, the author has obtained permission to reproduce the ads. Company representatives sometimes requested that a specific credit line be added to the photo caption; I have complied with those requests. In other cases, to simplify matters and to avoid large amounts of repetitive credit lines, I have omitted specific credit lines that indicate that the ad has been reproduced courtesy of a company or with their permission. However, the lack of a published credit line with each ad does not imply that permission wasn't obtained, or that the ads are in the public domain. The companies retain copyright protection for their trade-

"At ease...for refreshment"

There's something about the soda fountain... something inviting. And there's something about ice-cold "Coca-Cola"...a delicious taste...an after-sense of refreshment. No wonder you hear so often those passwords to a delightful experience..."Coca-Cola," or the friendly abbreviation, "Coke."

5¢

Hello... I'm "Coca-Cola" known, too, as "Coke"

8

Introduction

Orange explosions rip the air. Soldiers fling grenades and crawl under barbed wire. The landing signal officer on an aircraft carrier waves in a Hellcat that is flying on fumes. Anti-aircraft gun batteries pound incoming enemy planes. Back home, guys in uniform drink sodas and flirt with girls at store counters. Mothers ride bikes to the grocery store (saving gasoline); fathers grow potatoes in victory gardens. You'd expect to see these dramatic snapshots in World War II documentaries or newsreels, but they appeared in an unlikely source: magazine advertisements.

Wartime ads were both intimate and wide-ranging. They informed, entertained, and encouraged the folks at home. They also documented the transformation of American industry; some of the most famous brands in America abandoned stores and headed out to the front lines. The ads showed the effects that the War Production Board (WPB) had on the American market-

place, revealing not only what the average citizen did during the war, but also what famous companies did.

The ads offered a much wider spectrum of approaches and techniques to convey information about the war than any other source of information. They used humor and satire, and didn't hesitate to play on the viewer's emotions. In an information package about the Sixth War Loan, the Office of War Information (OWI) described the foe this way: "Slimy, treacherous, venomous, crafty, tough—that's the kind of enemy we've got to lick in the Pacific."

Wartime ads contained images of aircraft and combat that were as accurate as any painting or illustration of the time. Spurred and focused by official agencies such as the OWI and such volunteer groups as the War Advertising Council, the ads blended patriotism with propaganda. Sometimes they were sensitive, and at other times they were blunt. They ranged from strikingly effective to corny and silly. In searching for truth and objectivity, students of the war will find that ads offer a wealth of material for study.

It is unfortunate that advertising's vision of the war, so new and surprising then, is nearly ignored and forgotten today. There are several reasons for this neglect, but primarily it's because most people look at ads as a source of propaganda, not journalism. Readers and critics alike discount advertising as a source of anything meaningful.

Furthermore, homefront advertising seems an unlikely source of insight. During the war, the nation's focus stayed on the guys at the front, and after the war, the guys who dodged the bullets and flew the planes wrote moving books about their experiences. No

Navy dive bombers—about to strike! In each rear cockpit rides a radio gunner —trusted protector of his pilot and plane. His skill with radio and detection devices permits his pilot to concentrate on flying the plane and blasting the objective. His marksmanship makes enemy planes scarcer, brings V-Day nearer.

Hats Off to Naval Aircrewmen!

They're the highly trained Radiomen, Machinist's Mates or Ordnancemen who man rear or turret guns in dive bombers, torpedo bombers and multi-engined planes. By their combat record of skill, bravery and unfailing teamwork, they've won their place among the Navy's finest! *Back them up—by buying more War Bonds!*

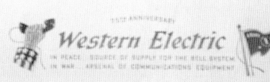

75TH ANNIVERSARY

Western Electric

IN PEACE... SOURCE OF SUPPLY FOR THE BELL SYSTEM
IN WAR... ARSENAL OF COMMUNICATIONS EQUIPMENT

amount of praise for the sacrifices and hardships of the folks back home could shift the spotlight. Although there are several excellent accounts of life on the homefront, most of the books about the war deal with combat. Compared to combat, life at home seemed mundane, and compared to formal histories of the war, advertisements seem trivial and ephemeral.

Yet, advertising during the war was pervasive. Roland Marchand points out in his book *Advertising the American Dream*, "Few images have buffeted the consciousness of twentieth-century Americans as repetitively as advertisements." When critics of advertising question not only its validity but its effectiveness, they are keeping open a debate that is far from settled. As Marchand argues, "We may not be able to prove the specific effect of an advertisement on its readers, but neither can we prove the effects of religious tracts, social manifestos, commemorative addresses, and political campaign speeches on their audiences." Some ads missed the target, he admits, but "advertisers still tested the effects of their communications more often and more rigorously than novelists, writers of magazine fiction, newspaper editors, movie directors, cartoonists or even politicians."

Wartime advertising was also controversial; there were full-blown arguments about whether it should even be permitted. But the ads remained popular. Surveys found that soldiers liked looking at the ads because the pretty girls, morale-boosting tableaux, and other vivid pictures reminded them of life back home.

Stateside, the war was altering the newspapers and magazines that people read, the places they worked and the jobs they did, and the ideas they thought about and discussed. It changed the cars they drove to the store and what they bought once they got there. It revolutionized priorities and habits.

In popular American media in 1940, the hint of world war was a distant rumor, a troubling sort of thunder on the horizon that most citizens hoped or imagined would not come close. In two years, everything changed. News stories now concentrated on events at the front: "After the landing, Allies advance across the flatlands at Anzio," a headline announced. Articles dealt with such topics as "Truscott of the 7th" and "Torpedo Bombers—They Are the Aerial Scourge of Ships." War-related trends were news, too; a typical article from *Life* magazine was entitled "Food Garden" and included a chart that "will help you grow 16 vegetables," the magazine promised. In August 1942, *Life* ran an article called "A Tank Arsenal: How Its Assembly Lines Operate," with a huge, detailed, two-page illustration.

American companies had already felt the effects of the demands of national defense and the Lend-Lease Act. In April 1941, as American industry was rolling into high gear, the demands of wartime production had already spread an intricate network throughout the country. By January 1944, the US Army Air Force (AAF) would have expended 40 million rounds of ammo; someone had to manufacture it.

Many companies retained few of their existing products. By 1942, Caterpillar was producing only seventeen of the fifty-four pieces of equipment that it usually made. Other firms converted completely. An appliance factory started producing gun mounts for tanks. A heater company made machine gun tripods. A brake plant made fuzes. A stamping shop turned out anti-tank mines. Many of these changes were documented with wartime advertisements.

Conversion for war was physical and psychological. A tall, wire fence was erected around the Maytag plant in Iowa; guards checked everyone going in and out. "These workers produced for war in a plant which had been so completely converted that a visitor could not have recognized it as the same one which formerly produced Maytag washers," a company history said.

Buick's Plant 11, where 234,083 automobile engines had been made, turned out its last one on February 3, 1942. Six days later, the peacetime equipment began moving out. "It was not an easy thing for Buick men to watch," the authors of *The Buick—A Complete History* wrote. "Patriotism mingled with a sort of emptiness, a knot in the stomach as production lines and installations which had taken years to develop and perfect were ripped out. . . . In a scant two weeks, the proud engine assembly line was a memory."

Behind the efforts of the Automotive Council for War Production, representing dozens of major automotive factories that converted to making tanks and planes, were thousands of suppliers of parts and equipment. For example, in Indianapolis, one auto company was producing 400 high-speed aircraft engines per month. The main fabricated and semi-finished parts in the engines came from smaller manufacturers in thirty-four cities. Magnetic plugs came from Clarinda, Iowa. Bronze units came from East Alton, Illinois, bearings from Stamford, Connecticut, distributors from Sidney, New York, and ignition assemblies from Warren, Ohio.

Closer examination showed that the chain stretched even farther. For the company in Warren, Ohio, to assemble the ignition systems, fifty-two other companies in a score of cities and towns had to contribute parts and supplies. From Edenton, North Carolina, and LaGrange, Georgia, came cotton yarn for the wiring. Cable markers came from Irvington, New Jersey, castor oil from New York City, small tools from a tool-and-die shop in Greenfield, Massachusetts, and acid tanks from a company in St. Louis.

In all of these shops, the workers who were building what President Roosevelt called the "arsenal of democracy" were punching time clocks, putting in

Next page
This May 1944 ad contrasts the comforts of home with the battle front, a frequent theme of wartime ads—and makes a pitch for war bonds. It also anticipates the end of the war, a note struck increasingly often in late 1944 and early 1945.
Courtesy, The General Electric Hall of History Foundation

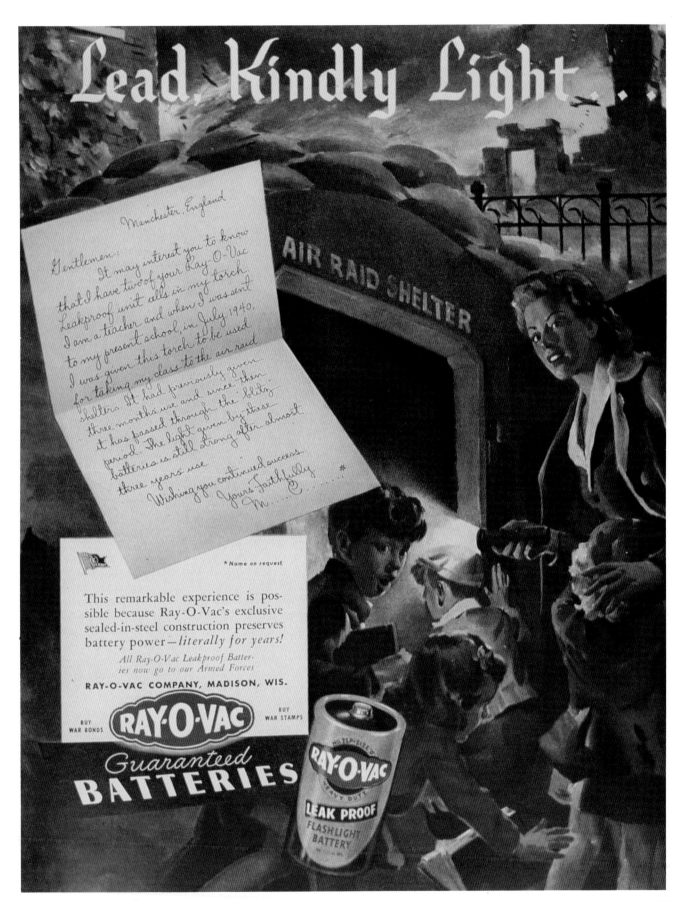

13

overtime, working harder and faster, and identifying with the soldiers, sailors, and marines for whom they were making weapons and equipment.

Some products lacked glamor, but played surprisingly important roles—Caterpillar's tractors, for example. In a company history called *Caterpillar—Century of Change*, editor Tom Biederbeck quoted Admiral William "Bull" Halsey, who commanded the navy in the Pacific: "The four machines that won the war in the Pacific were the submarine, radar, the airplane and the bulldozer."

Familiar companies did surprising tasks. Goodyear's balloon experts (who made giant, comic balloons for New York's Thanksgiving Day parades) created dummy versions of amphibious craft, PT boats, tanks, and artillery. The balloons were part of the "phantom fleet," used to confuse German air reconnaissance before D-day. The replicas were inflated, then deflated and moved by truck during the night. Some 600 Goodyear employees worked on the top-secret project.

Companies participated in less direct ways, too. AT&T, Studebaker, divisions of General Motors, General Foods, Western Electric, and A&P (the Atlantic & Pacific Tea Company) sent executives to government boards and agencies. Others went to Washington in humanitarian roles. In July 1942, when President Roosevelt appointed a War Relief Control Board to try to sort out the myriad war-relief causes and their relative importance, he included Gerard Swope of General Electric and Ralph Hayes, vice president of Coca-Cola.

In their ads, companies quickly began to trumpet their contributions to the war effort. The content and tone of their annual reports contained similar messages. The General Foods 1942 report declared, "To those

who fight on far-flung battle fronts, to our allies, to those who also serve on farms, in homes, or at machines and desks and counters, to those who struggle for our victory and peace, *Food* is a prime necessity. As one small part of the vast and vital industry of food, faced now with its greatest challenge, we as a corporation pledge ourselves to make our utmost contribution."

The effects of the war on American businesses weren't related only to production, and weren't always obvious. Overseas factories and subsidiaries were in combat zones. "Japanese bombers and invaders destroyed buildings, records and supplies of Franklin Baker Company of the Philippines, at Banahaw, on December 29, 1941. The plant had been vacated a few days earlier," the 1941 report from General Foods noted. It also pointed out that one of the company's fishing trawlers had been chartered by the government for a month, and seven others had been commandeered.

The company's 1942 report had grim news: "In May, a U-boat surfaced off one of the North Atlantic fishing banks. It sank one of our fishing trawlers. One member of the 17-man crew was killed by shellfire." In August, another trawler was sunk. The report also noted that the company's bag plant was producing sandbags for the army, and that 1,480 employees (14.5 percent of the total) had joined the armed forces.

In May 1942, Kraft's employee newsletter, *Cheesekraft*, printed the name of every employee in uniform. Wrapped around a message from J. L. Kraft, the list took four pages; the first page started with L. C. Abbenhouse of Seattle and ended with Pvt. J. G. Crane of Medford, Oregon. The names—Crosetti, Fitzpatrick, Jones, Matursevitch, Desparois, Fritzenmeier—filled two more pages.

Those Americans who didn't enlist were bombarded with messages. Advertisements took on the trappings of combat and sacrifice. They served as a unifying factor: persuading, encouraging, selling new habits and ideas. "Don't go for that Sunday drive," the ads would say, "save your tires, instead." A new cast of characters moved in: the black market cheat, the spunky soldier's wife, the "soldier of production" (male and female). New themes took center stage: rationing, salvage drives, war bond sales. The ads boosted morale and taught millions of Americans new ways to "back the attack."

When the Allies started winning, ads kept them from getting complacent. As Elmer Davis, director of the OWI, said in September 1943, "Overoptimism makes people slacken up—makes them, as the President put it the other night, settle back in their rocking chairs and get ready to start the celebration, instead of going on doing the things which, if we keep doing them long enough, will make the celebration possible."

Before the war, nutrition information came from doctors or dieticians. During the war, it came from Uncle Sam himself, via *Uncle Sam's Food Guide*, produced by the Office of Defense Health and Welfare Services. That guide's advice appeared in one Kraft ad

Previous page

Thomas Garver, company historian for Ray-O-Vac Corporation, calls this ad "perhaps the best ad that Ray-O-Vac ran during the war." Although the air-raid threat was much more serious in England (site of this ad's scenario), flashlights were a hot item stateside, too. According to Lee Kennett, in his book For the Duration, *"the first blackouts spawned a 'run' on flashlights and batteries so pronounced that OPA had put ceiling prices on them." Ray-O-Vac's roots reach back to the French Battery Company, incorporated in January 1906. In February 1942, one division of the company joined with five other companies (that made such items as sporting goods, addressing machines, and books) to make Browning Automatic Rifles, eventually producing almost 172,000. Ray-O-Vac made the distinctive right-angle light, a flashlight with a 90-degree bend, for the Signal Corps. The company also made 8.2 million parts for anti-tank bazookas and 1.8 million parts for anti-tank grenades, and delivered a total of 293.4 million Leak Proof batteries to the military, and 250 million cells of other types. "While its normally colorful jacket was replaced by the military's olive drab, the Signal Corps permitted 'Ray-O-Vac' to be imprinted on each battery—a promotional plus which made the company name familiar to servicemen and women all over the globe," a company history noted. Reproduced by permission, Rayovac Corp.*

Headlines in the May-
tag Plant Newspaper
tell news highlights
of the war time years.

Once war erupted, employee newsletters were swept up in the tide of new topics and new themes that transformed all media. The inset issue of the "Maytag Bomber Drive Bulletin" is dated July 1, 1943. That issue contains a headline "'Buy-A-Bomber' Drive Begins"; the drive encouraged workers to buy war bonds through payroll deductions. The drive was successful, ending in the "purchase" of a B-26, nicknamed the Maytag Marauder, *which went into combat with 12 Squadron of the South African Air Force. The aircraft went on 19 successful missions over Africa, Sicily, and Italy before being ditched in the Mediterranean (the crew was saved). Courtesy, Maytag Co.*

Six months after Pearl Harbor, the front page of the Kraft employee newsletter, Cheesekraft, *left no doubt as to that company's commitment. Stirring words, gung-ho headlines— and "ads" for war bonds and the Red Cross. Courtesy, Kraft General Foods, Inc.*

in this way: "Uncle Sam says, 'Eat Cheese! Eat vegetables!'"

In some cases, advertisements spoke directly to workers. More often, ads targeted women, who were the usual homefront consumers, a role that was even more typical during the war, although many women took jobs outside the home and some entered the military. "The work of the housewife is seemingly so simple, so regular, so obvious, so trivial that it goes unnoticed, unrecorded, and unappreciated," D'Ann Campbell pointed out in her book *Women at War with America—Private Lives in a Patriotic Era.* Her statement does not hold true for wartime ads, in which women play a starring role.

Ultimately, what sets the ads of the war apart isn't their characters or their themes or their slogans. War-

time ads were more than "tin to win" campaigns and candy bars from home, just as the war was more than tactics and maneuvers and new kinds of fighter aircraft. The wartime ads unabashedly reflected what people accepted as the meaning of the war: preserving democracy and a way of life.

In his 1941 book *The American Cause,* Archibald MacLeish wrote, "What the enemies of liberty would have us take the word to mean is something men and money and machines created in the nineteenth century and *called* democracy—a way of owning property, a scheme of doing business, an opportunity for comfort or for power or for certain forms of gain or entertainment. . . . If democracy is what the fascists say it is—if

Next page
Many well-established advertisers seemed to slip effortlessly into wartime themes. In some cases, the people in the ad simply put on uniforms. Shortages of sugar added to the wartime appeal of candy bars; M&M's chocolate candy was included in C-ration kits because the candy shell could resist high temperatures. Courtesy, Mars, Inc.

16

"MOM..."

He was a thorn in their side . . .

All morning long, his accurate mortar fire kept them from forming up, smashed their supply trucks, broke the spearhead of their attack . . .

So, they went all out to get him . . .
And finally, a sniper shot him.

Then they laid down a cross fire that was death to defy. I know . . . because one of our men tried. But it was damned hard to lie there and hear him call "Mom" . . . and cry and call "Mom" again . . . like a kid who'd been hurt, he didn't know just how or why.

And all we could do was just lie there . . . and grind our teeth together and tighten our guts because each time he cried "Mom" . . . it tore out our insides.

When I couldn't stand it any more, I got up and ran . . .

And when they saw me coming and the Red Cross band of the Medical Corps on my arm, they held their fire until I knelt down beside him. I put a syrette into his arm and then another, and he relaxed and his head fell back and his eyes were still wide but I could tell he thought his mother was there by his side . . .

Listen, America . . .

Open your hearts, wives and daughters! Open your pocketbooks, fathers! Give your blood, brothers and sisters! Give your money . . . give your work!

So the freedom you want . . .
So the country you want . . .

So the future you want . . .
Will be there when we come back.

* * *

Here at Nash-Kelvinator we're building Pratt & Whitney engines for the Navy's Vought Corsairs and Grumman Hellcats . . . Hamilton Standard propellers for United Nations bombers . . . governors, binoculars, parts for ships, jeeps, tanks and trucks . . . readying production lines for Sikorsky helicopters. All of us devoted 100% to winning this war . . . to speeding the peace when our men will come back to their jobs and homes and even better futures than they had before . . . to the day when we'll build for you an even finer Kelvinator, an even greater Nash!

NASH-KELVINATOR CORPORATION
Kenosha · Milwaukee · DETROIT · Grand Rapids · Lansing

GIVE MORE HOURS!
BUY MORE WAR BONDS!
GIVE MORE BLOOD!

NASH
AUTOMOBILES
KELVINATOR
REFRIGERATORS · ELECTRIC RANGES

democracy is nothing but the world of innumerable automobiles and the best telephone system on earth and a new gadget just around the corner and the radios driveling on in the hotel lobbies eighteen hours out of twenty-four and the simpering legs in the magazine advertisements and the simpering voices on the movie screen and the hundreds of thousands of miles of roadside billboard faces and the ten millions of unemployed waiting for the next boom—if democracy is only this, then democracy cannot survive attack, for democracy is not a cause that men will fight for."

The purposes and achievements of World War II increasingly defined twentieth-century democracy, yet the accretions of memoirs and historical narratives muddle as often as they clarify. According to Paul Fussell, in his book *Wartime—Understanding and Behavior in the Second World War,* "For the past fifty years the Allied war has been sanitized and romanticized almost beyond recognition by the sentimental, the loony patriotic, the ignorant, and the bloodthirsty." This sanitizing was obvious in some wartime ads (as was censorship in wartime news releases from the government), yet there were plenty of no-nonsense, grim ads to balance the scales, especially later in the war.

Although MacLeish derided advertisements, their vocabulary and attitudes remain a rich, primary source of information about how contemporary Americans felt about the war, democracy, and capitalism. The ads offer peculiar insight into the team effort that was taking place back home, into what the soldiers were protecting, and what they were so anxious to come home to.

"Until I Come Back . . ."

The Nash-Kelvinator Corporation of Detroit led the way in producing gutsy, dramatic snapshots of the war in the illustrations and text of its domestic advertisements. This ad is a textbook example of how to use anecdotes, striking details, and plain language.

We're over 20,000 feet now (the coffee's frozen in the thermos) and that's the Zuyder Zee below. We must be halfway across Holland.

Funny thing what happens to a fellow . . .

Those are the same old stars and the same old moon that the girl and I were looking at last summer.

And here I am—flying 300 miles an hour in a bubble of glass, with ten tons of T.N.T.

Somehow—this isn't the way I imagined it at all, the day I enlisted. Don't get me wrong—sure I was sore at the Japs and the Nazis—but mostly, it was the thrill of the Great Adventure.

Well, I know now—the real reasons—why I'm up here paying my first call on Hitler.

It's only when you get away from the U.S.A. that you find out what the shootin's really about and what you're fighting for.

I learned from that Czech chap in London. The refugee, the nice old fellow who reminded me of Dad except for the maimed hands. I was dumb enough to ask about it. "I got that," he said, "for writing a book the Nazis didn't like . . ."

Then there was the captured German pilot who screamed and spit when Izzy Jacobs offered him a cigarette . . . how do fellows get that way?

And that crazy Polish pilot—the fellow who rammed the Messerschmitt. After the funeral I learned what was eating him. Seems as how he has a sister in Warsaw who had been sent to a German Officers' Club . . .

I hope to hell Hitler's home tonight . . . light and wind are perfect.

Yes, sir, I've met 'em by the dozens over here—guys warped by hate—guys who have had the ambition beaten out of them—guys who look at you as if you were crazy when you tell 'em what America is like.

They say America will be a lot different after this war.

Well, maybe so.

But as for me, I know the score . . . you learn fast over here. I know now there's only one decent way to live in this world—the way my folks lived and the way I want to live.

When you find a thing that works as good as that—brother, be careful with that monkey-wrench.

And there's one little spot—well, if they do as much as change the smell of the corner drug store—I will murder the guy.

I want my girl back, just as she is, and that bungalow on Maple Avenue . . .

I want that old roll-top desk of mine at the electric company, with a chance to move upstairs, or quit if I want to.

I want to see that old school of mine, and our church, just as they are—because I want my kids to go there.

That's *my home town* . . .

Keep it for me the way I remember it, just the way I see it now—until I come back.

Right on the beam for wartime eating!

Rice Krispies give you lots of vitamins and minerals. Delicious. Always ready. So CRISP they **snap! crackle! pop!**

★ America's crispest breakfast favorite takes on added duties these days. Delicious, golden Rice Krispies are the quick, easy way to give the family good nutrition they'll cheer at any meal, any hour. Always ready—they save time, work and fuel. They save other foods, too.

Rice Krispies are rich with whole grain food values in thiamin (Vitamin B₁), niacin and iron. Oven-popped to a crunchy crispness. Toasted to a mellow, golden brown. Rice Krispies boast a flavor that only an exclusive Kellogg recipe can give.

Tomorrow enjoy the lasting crispness of Rice Krispies at breakfast. Hear them snap! crackle! pop! Use these crunchy tempters often—at other meals, too.

"Rice Krispies" is a trade mark (Reg. U. S. Pat. Off.) of Kellogg Company for its oven-popped rice.

MADE BY KELLOGG'S IN BATTLE CREEK

U.S. NEEDS US STRONG
THIS TYPE OF FOOD IS AMONG THOSE RECOMMENDED IN THE NUTRITION FOOD RULES
EAT NUTRITIONAL FOOD

Kellogg's **RICE KRISPIES** OVEN-POPPED RICE WITH SUGAR SALT AND MALT FLAVORING MADE BY KELLOGG CREEK, MICH.

SAVE TIME—   SAVE FUEL—   SAVE WORK!

Minus regulation headgear, Kellogg's elves fly in formation to carry a wartime message. Snap, Crackle, and Pop were among dozens of familiar American trademarks that enlisted in the war effort, spreading the word about conservation and other themes. Note the Uncle Sam silhouette on the "U.S. Needs Us Strong" card by the plate, as well as the star-spangled tablecloth. Courtesy, Kellogg Co.

19

"Thank God for Americans with FIGHTING BLOOD"

All day they've been bringing in the wounded. And now her practiced hands work almost automatically. Again she reaches for the precious plasma—again an arm is bared to receive it—again a failing pulse grows stronger—again a soldier is saved from death to come back home.

As this army nurse sees the power of plasma, is it any wonder she breathes a prayer of thanks that it is there in time? And her thanks are echoed by officers and men of the medical corps—by thousands of wounded on hospital cots—by all the mothers who wait

and hope. Life-saving plasma is made from blood—blood donated by Americans who take this means of putting themselves in the fight with their fighting men. It's the kind of blood that has built America—the kind of blood that has kept her free—*fighting blood!* As the

war continues to grow in intensity, we must give more and more. We dare not fail. Why not call your Red Cross Blood Donor Center and make an appointment today? Belmont Radio Corporation, 5923 West Dickens Avenue, Chicago 39, Illinois.

Belmont Radio
TELEVISION ★ F.M. ★ ELECTRONICS

Chapter 1

Life On The Homefront

"Have You Any Magazines That Are Not Full Of War Stories?"

To understand the verbal and visual vocabularies of the advertisements of the early 1940s, you have to understand the events and popular attitudes of the years just before the war. Emotional appeals, new stereotypes, and surprising images burst upon the usually predictable pages of American magazines. Where did they come from? Why were they there?

Since the ads were aimed at consumers, their central focus was on the habits and expectations of shoppers and readers. The Depression was not so distant, and the American economy seemed to be finally firing on all cylinders. No one was anxious to let international politics throw a monkey wrench into the transmission by diverting welcome consumer goods into perhaps unneeded weapons. Although war was festering in Europe, there was nothing approaching popular support for it here at home. Folks looked back to World War I with a sense of *deja vu,* and asked themselves what had been accomplished. If the choice was between a new sedan for the family or a tank for the Russians, many Americans found it easy to choose the former.

At the same time, the country had clearly entered a period of rearmament in September 1939, when President Roosevelt declared a state of "limited emergency." This warm-up period did not command the media spotlight as did the total war to follow. Looking at the ads of 1939 and 1940, war still seemed a remote possibility.

The distance soon began to shrink dramatically—and not just in the news of the world. President Roosevelt, convinced that we'd enter the war sooner or later,

James Montgomery Flagg's Uncle Sam poster, familiar during both world wars, was already a national icon by the time General Electric borrowed the theme for this September 1942 ad. While many companies trumpeted their specific contributions to war production, GE took a mysterious approach in the italicized copy at bottom right: "The volume of General Electric war production is so high and the degree of secrecy required is so great that we cannot tell you about it now," a typical wartime ad said. "When it can be told we believe the story of industry's developments during the war years will make one of the most fascinating chapters in the history of industrial progress." Courtesy, The General Electric Hall of History Foundation

Previous page
In March 1944, Belmont Radio focused on a wartime role of women and made a plea for blood donors. This ad could have also been a recruiting call for the Cadet Nurse Corps, which recruited 65,291 women during the war. According to one source, 40 percent of them were attracted by a single series of magazine advertisements.

As early as 1940, the Association of American Railroads operated an extremely active public relations program, an effort that would result in ads such as this one after the war started. In its 1940 annual report, the Association pointed out that the commercial air-transport and motor-trucking industries had embarked on similar programs. This November 1942 ad tells consumers to travel only when necessary. If Nike had been around during the war, its ads would have had to say, "Just don't do it." Courtesy, Association of American Railroads

This ad blends news (in the form of photos and stories about actual aircrew members) and advertising in a way that was common during the war, when some ad designers sought no-nonsense approaches.

ordered a general mobilization of the national guard and the navy and Marine Corps reserves in the summer of 1940. That September, Congress passed the Selective Service Act, the first American peacetime draft.

Within a year, nearly a dozen American merchant ships had been sunk by warring nations, two American warships had been attacked, and more than 100 Americans had been killed in the process. Although it took Pearl Harbor to finally propel us into declaring war, we were already primed and ready. Recruiting stations stayed open on the Sunday after Pearl Harbor to handle the thousands of soldiers-to-be for whom the Japanese attack was the final straw.

One month after Pearl Harbor, the army announced that it would double in size. The Selective Service System expanded to cover men from twenty to forty-four years old. Gradually, men (and even a few

women) in khaki, olive drab and navy blue became a regular sight in American cities and towns.

By the end of 1941, "The reminders of the war were everywhere," veteran Donald Rogers later wrote in his book *Since You Went Away.* Rogers' comment applies to advertising, as well. The currents that surged through society were echoed and reflected in the ad pages of magazines and newspapers.

The folks at home felt a welter of emotions. They were furious at the Japanese and the Germans. Although basically confident in American strength, they were dejected by the headlines that painted a grim picture of Allied failure on all fronts. They were determined to do their share, but confused about exactly what that meant. They were afraid of spies, enemy sabotage, and even enemy air raids (a Gallup poll in

Next page
Advertisements seem an unlikely source of war news, but this March 1944 pitch from the AAF boasts of real battles and a real B–26.

One More on the Nose!

A fighting flier wears his decorations on his chest. But a fighting plane wears *hers* on her nose.

And one look at the bombs and Swastikas painted on this B-26—"The Exterminator"—will tell you she's a two-fisted fightin' fool!

Like the notches on an old-time Injun-fighter's gun, they keep track of her score. A bomb for everyone of her 40 successful missions . . . a Swastika for each of the six Nazi planes she's shot down.

"The Exterminator" fought her way through some of the war's hottest actions. She blasted Bizerte,

Tunis, Sousse, Pantelleria, Sardinia, Naples and Rome. She "exterminated" the Germans' bridges, shattered their railroad yards, skip-bombed their ships. She pounded Salerno for a week to help pave the way for the 5th Army's landing.

Yet on all these flights, in all these fights, *not a man in her crew was scratched*. That's the kind of fighting record that makes bad reading in Berlin!

And that's the kind of team *you'll* be on when you fly with the A.A.F. . . . the hardest-hitting, best-trained team that ever took to the sky!

Bombardier, Navigator, Pilot, Gunner . . . whatever wings you wear . . . you'll hit the enemy often, and hit him hard. And you'll know how to get back home, so you can hit him again tomorrow.

And the Swastikas, or Rising Suns, painted on the nose of *your* plane, will be plenty of proof that you, too, are part of the "greatest team in the world!"

U. S. ARMY RECRUITING SERVICE

40 MISSIONS—NOBODY SCRATCHED

Every Bombardier, every Navigator, every Pilot, every Gunner who wears A. A. F. wings, gets training unequalled by that of any air force in the world . . . training that makes him a better flier and a better fighter than the enemy he meets.

FLY AND FIGHT WITH THE

AAF
ARMY AIR FORCES

GREATEST TEAM IN THE WORLD

The "Rambler" Roars into Rangoon

This morning you're flying with the crew of the famous "Rangoon Rambler"...

Crouched in the glassed-in nose beside you, Lt. Guy Sports, the navigator, studies a map spread across his knees, checks off landmarks as they slide past underneath. Suddenly he peers ahead... speaks into his throat-microphone: "Pilot from navigator. There she is, Rote. We can see the target now. Alter course to three-three-zero."

"Roger!" Capt. Raymond Rote, the pilot, eases the big B-24 around and straightens out on his new course.

Then you see it... a splash of flame against the green horizon..., the great, gold-domed Shwe Dagon Pagoda that towers over Rangoon. You're getting close... and the crew gets set. Lt. Robert Currie, the bombardier, fiddles with the knobs on his bombsight. Capt. Gordon Wilson, co-pilot, gives the instruments a last-minute check.

Now you're over the target..., a flock of pot-bellied Jap cargo ships squatting there in the river's bend. The "Rambler" lurches and bucks as she ducks through bursts of ack-ack and goes into her bombing run.

Your heart pounds hard. Then Currie comes in on the intercom... cool as if he were ordering cokes at the Assam Officers Club: "Pilot from bombardier, Bombs away! Let's get out of here, pal!"

Looking back and below, you watch the formation's bombs bullseye the target. A freighter goes up in a blast of fire and black smoke. The ship beside it explodes. Flames break out from a third. And a fourth. Currie and the other bombardiers were "on the beam" today.

Rote banks the Lib around steep, and you high-tail for home. You're congratulating yourself when... "Fighters at four o'clock—high!" somebody yells. You look up and see a formation of Japs sweeping out of the sun.

Now it's the gunners' turn. And between squirts of their big, twin-50's they keep up a running pep-talk:

"There goes his wing down! He's coming in! This one's *my* meat, Salley!"

"Hey, skipper—kick her over a little, I want a good shot at this guy."

And two Japs spiral down in flames, and the rest decide to quit. That's all for today. You look around at the crew, relaxing now, shooting the breeze, adding up the score. You think of the ribbons each man has won for flights like this.

And it makes your chest puff out with pride to be flying with guys like these,...to be wearing the wings of the A.A.F.—the "greatest team in the world!"

U. S. ARMY RECRUITING SERVICE

THE "RANGOON RAMBLERS": Standing: Sgt. Ferdinand Knechtel, gunner; Capt. Raymond Rote; Capt. Gordon Wilson; Lt. Guy Sports; Lt. Robert Currie; Sgt. Joseph Willis, gunner. Seated: Sgt. John Craigie, Sgt. Carl Paak, Sgt. Adolph Scolavino, Sgt. Edward Salley, gunners.

MEN OF 17

...if you want to fly on a team like the "Rangoon Ramblers"... as Navigator, Bombardier, Pilot or Gunner... go to your nearest Aviation Cadet Examining Board..., see if you can qualify for the Air Corps Enlisted Reserve. If you qualify, you will receive this insignia... but will not be called for training until you are 18 or over.

When called, your special aptitudes will be studied further to determine the type of training you will receive. For the A.A.F. carefully selects for each position on a combat crew the man best qualified for the job... and then adds the thorough training which makes this all-star team the world's finest.

For pre-aviation training, see your local Civil Air Patrol officers. Also see your High School Principal or Adviser about recommended courses in the Air Service Division of the High School Victory Corps.

(Essential workers in war industry or Agriculture—do not apply.)

KEEP 'EM FLYING! For information on Naval Aviation Cadet Training, apply at nearest Office of Naval Officer Procurement. This advertisement has the approval of the Joint Army Navy Personnel Board.

FLY AND FIGHT WITH THE **AAF** ARMY AIR FORCES GREATEST TEAM IN THE WORLD

December 1941 found that half the country expected air attacks).

The wartime ads experimented with ways to guide, motivate, and reassure people. As with the official government pronouncements of the Office of Civil Defense, advertisers were uncertain about their approach. If they painted a grim, realistic picture, people might get depressed. If they seemed too upbeat, folks might get complacent. The result was an emotional hodgepodge.

Put yourself in the position of a homeowner in November 1942, reading an ad from the Hartford Insurance Company. It offers "war damage insurance." The ad says, "It isn't a question of whether or not there is going to BE a bombing or an invasion. The question is how you would be fixed for insurance IF there WERE one.... Two incendiary bombs might start a conflagration that your regular fire insurance policy wouldn't cover." Would you buy the insurance?

Advertisers faced equally thorny questions, such as how to handle military recruiting. The military services needed men, of course, and fast. Plenty of ads encouraged people to enlist, portraying those who did as heroes. But factories and farms needed workers, too. If too many young men enlisted, who would be left to build howitzers and harvest wheat? So the ads showed the folks who stayed home as heroes, too. And in fact the question was moot; there was soon a national shortage of workers.

The Armstrong Cork Company had been providing military leaves of absence for its employees since before Pearl Harbor. All told, more than 5,000 Armstrong employees would serve in the armed forces during the war. Between 1940 and 1945, 3,000 General Foods employees (23 percent of the total) had joined the military. At the end of 1942, 4,286 employees of the National Dairy Products Corporation had entered the armed forces. Nine had been killed, and two were missing in action. In 1943, 2,080 more National Dairy employees entered the armed services, and "12 more gave their lives for their country, increasing the total number on our service flag to 6,366, and the gold stars to 21," the company's 1943 annual report said. Westinghouse had 70,000 employees at the beginning of the war; nearly 27,000 went into the service and 550 died in the line of duty.

From January 1 to October 31, 1942, 9,219 Ford employees entered the military services. "This made a mockery of the Ford effort to prepare workers in school and shop for their role in production," historians Allan Nevins and Frank Ernest Hill wrote in their book *Ford*. The gigantic Ford aircraft factory at Willow Run, which was initially infamous for missing its pro-

duction schedules, may have faced one of the most conspicuous examples of a shortage of workers. "The chief cause of slowness was lack of manpower," Nevins and Hill concluded. Expected to employ 90,000 people, it had only about 30,000 workers in January 1943. The work force would reach 42,300 that June, but turnover and absenteeism made it seem like less.

It's You . . . and the Rest of the Team

Your big Liberator is coming in fast now . . . boring head-on through black bursts of flak that rock her like a canoe. From your grandstand seat in the greenhouse, you can see fires down below. That's where the first wave laid its eggs. You're next!

Sometimes, back at "pre-flight", it didn't quite add up. Logarithms . . . formulas . . . classes all day. You couldn't see how you'd ever use the stuff they crammed into your head. But you stuck it out. You wanted Bombardier's wings.

The top-turret guns begin to spit, as you hunch down over your bombsight. Check for altitude! Check for air-speed! The guns are going faster now, but you won't let yourself look up. Check for wind-drift! Suddenly you realize you're doing things automatically . . . all the things that came so hard in training. And you're doing them right!

In advanced school you got pretty cocky. Pilots? Navigators? O. K. for some guys maybe. But you're the man they build bombers around! You pack the knock-out punch!

The Lib heels, and straightens out on her target, and Pete comes in over the interphone: "O. K. Slugger. She's yours. Make it good!" You're the boss now. This is what you've been waiting for. You glue your eye to the sight, and talk into your throat microphone: "Level, Pete . . . hold that level. Bomb-bay doors open. Left a little . . . level now . . . level . . . perfect!" And there's your target—caught in the cross-hairs like a fly in a spider web.

You jab the release. *"Bombs Away!"*

Now you've done it! The seconds drag out . . . and then Beezy, back at the tail-gun, yells: "HIT—HIT—HIT—HIT! On target!! Hey, Lieutenant. Come and get your cigar!"

Well . . . ! Your chest starts to swell . . . and then all at once you see that it wasn't just *you* who smeared that Nazi base. It was Pete, up in the pilot's seat . . . Cliff, with his navigation charts . . . the gunners, Jim, Tony, Beezy, Lou. It was you . . . and the *rest* of the crew . . . flying as a team . . .

The same kind of team that paved the way for the landings in the Gilberts . . . that cleaned up the Japs on Kiska . . . that flattened Bremen and Wilhelmshaven . . . that is carrying the war to Japan . . .

The A.A.F. . . . . the greatest team in the world!

U. S. ARMY RECRUITING SERVICE

MEN OF 17 . . .

You can get ready now for your place—as Bombardier, Navigator or Pilot—on this great A.A.F. team. Go to the nearest Aviation Cadet Examining Board . . . see if you can qualify for the Air Corps Enlisted Reserve. If you qualify, you will receive Enlisted Reserve insignia . . . but will not be called for training until you are 18 or over.

When called, you'll be given 5 months' training (after a brief conditioning period) in one of America's finest colleges . . . you'll get dual-control flying instruction . . . then go on to eight months of full flight training . . . the kind of training that makes America's fliers the world's best! When you graduate as a Bombardier, Navigator or Pilot — you will receive a $250 uniform allowance and your pay will be $246 to $327 per month.

Meanwhile, see your local Civil Air Patrol Officers about C.A.P. Cadet training . . . also your High School principal or adviser about recommended courses in the Air Service Division of the H. S. Victory Corps. Both afford valuable pre-aviation training.

(Essential workers in War Industry or Agriculture—do not apply.)

KEEP 'EM FLYING! *For information regarding Naval Aviation Cadet Training at the Naval Aviation Cadet Selection Board in any office of Officer Procurement, or at any Naval Recruiting Station; or, if you are in the Navy, Marine Corps or Coast Guard, apply through your commanding officer . . . This advertisement has the approval of the Joint Army Navy Personnel Board.*

FLY AND FIGHT WITH THE AAF *ARMY AIR FORCES* **GREATEST TEAM IN THE WORLD**

When 100,000 former workers traded their denim coveralls for khaki, navy blue and olive drab, home-front production managers had to find 200,000 replacements. Ads helped broadcast the pitch, luring retirees back to work, asking people who had jobs to moonlight, and convincing women to leave their kitchens for assembly lines. In 1943, General Foods set up special shifts at its factories for part-time workers: schoolboys and girls, clerks, housewives, and even salesmen.

Ray-O-Vac employed 600 German prisoners at its Milwaukee plant. Grumman's new workers included "butchers, bakers, brokers, housewives, clerks, farmers (many from Long Island's potato fields), clam-diggers, gravediggers, poets, policemen," wrote company historian Richard Thruelsen in *The Grumman Story*. Even federal prisoners got into the act, making bombs, cartridge clips, gun parts, and patrol boats; at San Quentin, they made submarine nets.

The authorities showed less creativity in the Soviet Union, where workers were simply drafted to run new industries. In 1941, one million Soviet housewives, students, and schoolchildren went to work in industrial plants and factories.

This illustration accompanies one of Caterpillar's ads, as another familiar trademark appeared in a combat zone—here, obviously the tropics. During World War II, the 497th Heavy Shop Company of the Army Engineers had many members who were former Caterpillar employees. The company helped build the Burma Road. The men called their maintenance camp "Little Peoria" (location of Caterpillar's headquarters) and gave every lane and building a Peoria name. Courtesy, Caterpillar, Inc.

In America, Ray-O-Vac established seven new plants and hired 14,000 new workers. The Madison, Wisconsin, Ray-O-Vac plant grew from 750 employees to 1,824, about two-thirds of whom were women. To get enough workers, Ray-O-Vac contacted churches, clubs, PTAs, ministers, and college professors. The company employed part-time office workers, off-duty policemen and firemen, students, injured servicemen from a nearby airfield, and housewives. People could work full time or a couple hours a day, on irregular schedules; they could show up, work a few hours and get paid right away.

During the first three years of the war, the Maytag payroll grew from 1,200 to more than 3,000. About one-third of these employees were women employed for the first time as production workers. The armed services drafted 557 employees. Wartime employment at Buick peaked at 44,600 workers, more than twice the pre-war number. In 1943, Lockheed reached its record high for employment: 94,000. In the fall of 1939, there were 3,900 employees at the Martin Aircraft Company. By the end of 1940, there were 13,000, and by Christmas 1942, nearly 53,000. At peak employment, nearly 35 percent were women.

In 1943, female employees increased 77 percent at Ford plants and 139 percent at General Motors plants.

In general, the proportion of female workers varied from about 5 percent to 20 percent. Caterpillar set up an aluminum foundry in East Peoria staffed by 85 percent women. By 1947, 16 million women employed outside the home constituted 28 percent of the work force. That percentage would continue to rise.

By 1944, an advertisement for the Pennsylvania Railroad could point out, "Today, on the Pennsylvania

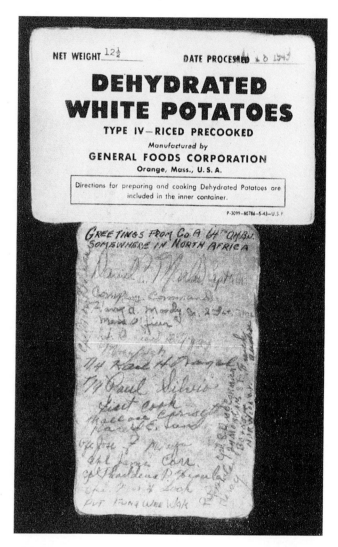

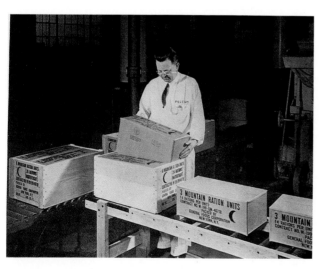

Employee newsletters were full of stories about how workers were contributing to the war effort. This photo appeared in the 1942 annual report from General Foods, with this caption: "This Postum employee is crating 2 cartons containing 24 individual watertight rations of the U.S. Army's 'Mountain Ration.' This is one of the many special combat rations developed by the U.S. Army Quartermaster Corps. In 1942 GF plants packed several special rations for the Government." Also among the 1944 products from General Foods were AAF flight packs, flight rations, four-in-one mountain rations, K-rations, Red Cross packs, and special chocolate and ration bars. Two GF shops were even making parts for bombers. In 1945, the company reported that its total production for the government during the war was $114.5 million. Courtesy, Kraft General Foods, Inc.

The original caption for this photo in the 1943 annual report from General Foods said: "Somewhere in North Africa Cpl. Morris Davis ate some excellent mashed potatoes and had a hunch they were the kind his mother makes at a GF plant somewhere in the U.S.A. A check-up with the mess sergeant proved him right so he and his buddies signed the box top which he sent home as a testimonial." Note the "greetings from somewhere in North Africa" headline, the classic wartime location. In 1943, General Foods sent 35 percent of its production of Birds Eye vegetables to the military services. For the military, the company also made such things as quick-cooking rice, dehydrated soups, and powdered drinks—all in generic-looking packages. Courtesy, Kraft General Foods, Inc.

Mine eyes have seen the glory . . .

My two brothers are in the Army. One in New Guinea. One a prisoner in Germany.

The man I'm going to marry is in the Army. Bomber pilot in Burma.

That's *their* contribution to freedom, *their* glory . . .

But what is mine?

To sit and wish for my men to come home? Or to want freedom so much that I, too, will go out and help make it come sooner?

Every hour I live, every day that slides swiftly away into the past, I'm thankful I'm a Wac . . .

Sharing the work of war with our soldiers. Learning to understand their innermost feelings about freedom and service. To be absorbed, as they are, in the Army of the United States.

I've seen, with my own eyes, that doing my own special Army job is the real way to share *their* honor, and *their* glory . . .

Now. And in the heaven of Victory to come.

———

For full information about the Women's Army Corps, go to your nearest U.S. Army Recruiting Station. Or mail the coupon at the right.

Good soldiers...

THE **WAC**

PAINTED BY SCHLAIKJER

The overt mention of a prisoner marks this recruiting ad as a late-war product; it appeared in October 1944. The artist, Jes William Schlaikjer, was a prolific designer of posters, as well.

Railroad, approximately 22,000 women are serving . . . we're glad to have their help in the greatest job railroads have ever been called on to do, moving men and materials to Victory!" An ad from a hand-cream maker would add, "The more women at war . . . the sooner we'll win!"

There had been 5.5 million unemployed Americans back in 1939; by 1944, only 670,000 weren't punching a time clock somewhere. The holdouts must have had either severe disabilities or equally severe allergies to labor.

The tremendous growth of wartime industry did much more than create Rosie the Riveter as a cultural icon and spur the use of daycare for kids. Some ads showed the downside of the worker shortage. An ad for motor oil showed a dejected businessman looking at a padlocked door on a local garage. "The padlock that makes Mr. Slocum shudder," the headline says. "Mr.

"Gangway! I've got a Sergeant waiting!"

In May 1944, Cannon boosted morale and made simultaneous pitches for conservation and war bonds. "For many wives, correspondence was just like keeping a diary," wrote D'Ann Campbell in Women at War with America. "*The main topics were daily activities, children, friends, families, past and future together, assurances of love, and general discussion of topics of mutual interest." In a Chicago study, 14 percent of the wives sent clippings, pictures, and packages. "A few felt inhibited from writing their intimate thoughts because they knew that censors read all letters," Campbell noted. Courtesy, Fieldcrest Cannon, Inc.*

Slocum hates that padlock on Smith's Car Repair Shop," the copy says. "He should. His car is eight years old—ripe for a breakdown. The town's only other mechanic is booked for weeks ahead. We're *all* in the same fix. The average car is over 7½ years old—and almost half our mechanics are gone. Repair work is piling up. Repair parts, too, are notably lacking."

The ad is interesting because it includes a small inset picture of what seems to be a newspaper clipping with the headline "Some Grim Facts on the Car Situation." The clipping says, "There are 22,000 fewer car repair shops today than the 108,000 we had at war's start. . . . And out of every 100 mechanics we had, only 47 are left. . . . If car manufacturing resumed tomorrow, it would take at least 4 years to fill the demand for new cars. . . ."

Because industry wasn't always located where the workers lived, tens of thousands of people had to relocate to new sections of the country. When they got there, they faced drastic housing shortages. Some situations were so extreme they were ridiculous. By May 1942, virtually no housing had been provided at Ford's gigantic Willow Run plant, although a work force of more than 50,000 employees was anticipated.

Many wives of servicemen followed their husbands from camp to camp until the soldiers were sent overseas. The living arrangements for these women were often squalid, ranging (according to one survey) from "pretty poor" to "very poor" for the wives of enlisted men. For those who remained back home, about half moved in with their parents or in-laws, instead of establishing their own homes.

In the ads, uprooted folks took their lot philosophically, if not cheerfully. And, later in the war, at least they could anticipate when it would be over. A 1944 General Electric ad, for example, shows a wife talking to her husband: "For almost a year, I've been traipsing around the country like some kind of a gypsy," she says. "I've set up housekeeping in a run-down hotel . . . in a threadbare rooming house . . . in a bleak tourist camp. I'm not complaining, though. I'd go through a lot worse than this . . . to be near a husband who may get his overseas orders any hour, any day . . . Well, living out of a suitcase has me sold on one thing. Come the peace, I want me a *home* where I can settle down for good." GE's logo has this line of type above it: "Everything Electrical For After-Victory Homes." At least in this ad, the family unit was still intact, if only tenuously. That wasn't the case for many displaced workers.

Next page
This May 1944 ad, like others that year, anticipated the end of hostilities, no doubt triggering similar dreams by soldiers on the front. Housing shortages were chronic near military posts and industrial centers. Artist Lyman Anderson also produced war posters, including a well-known one called "They'll Let Us Know When to Quit" for the War Manpower Commission. Courtesy, The General Electric Hall of History Foundation

"For almost a year, I've been traipsing around the country like some kind of a gypsy.

"I've set up housekeeping in a run-down hotel . . . in a threadbare rooming house . . . in a bleak tourist camp. I'm not complaining, though. I'd go through a lot worse than this . . . to be near a husband who may get his overseas orders any hour, any day.

"But I would certainly *love* to meet the guy who got off that remark about home being where you hang your hat!

"Home is where you hang your hat—MY EYE!"

"Well, living out of a suitcase has me sold on one thing. Come the peace, I want me a *home* where I can settle down for good . . . and I want it to have every last contrivance for taking the wear and tear out of living . . . and putting happiness in it.

"There's only one thing I want more. That's my husband . . . back again, safe and sound."

With young couples like this—with all who feel as they do—the people at General Electric see eye to eye. The first thing we want is Victory. That's why we're doing nothing but war work . . . making things, skillfully and carefully, to help bring fighting men back sooner, and bring them back sound.

Meantime, we are sharing your dreams for a home of your own.

We share them because, normally, our business is making all the electrical things that make a house a liveable, workable home. And because it is our aim to make your postwar home—no matter how modest a home it may be—a marvel of comfort and convenience through the use of electricity.

For example, you couldn't wish for a finer Electric Range than the one G.E. was making *before* the war. There's an oven that turns itself on—turns itself off—you can even fix it so a bell will ring when the food is ready. If you've ever used one of these amazing work-savers, you know that our dreams for your future home are based on the reality of things already perfected.

So you keep on buying War Bonds. They build up the purchasing power that will make jobs after the war . . . and help you pay for that after-victory home.

Everything Electrical For After-Victory Homes

GENERAL ⓖⓔ ELECTRIC

RANGE

WORKPOWER

IS ON OUR SIDE

When the Japs struck, they had built up such superiority in manpower, firepower and airpower, that early victories came with astonishing ease. But they had one blind spot. On quickly conquered islands where it became necessary to build airfields and defenses, their tools were pitifully inadequate — picks and shovels, baskets and little ricksha carts!

On the Allied side was a weapon they had overlooked — *workpower* — the husky American earth-moving machines that overcome the handicap of time.

A high-ranking U. S. Army officer has called the track-type Diesel tractor one of the three "most valuable weapons of warfare." Along with the jeep and the cargo plane, this heavy-duty weapon-of-all-work has given our fighting men the vital edge of victory — not once, but many times. For neither Germany nor Japan has any comparable equipment.

The men who drive the big Diesels built a lifeline chain of island bases to Australia in the eleven terrible weeks after Pearl Harbor, and had a bomber field ready on Umnak in time to save Alaska.

"Bulldozers," they call those tireless machines. Engineers and Seabees use the name in their letters home. War correspondents and radio commentators apply it to any war tractor, whether equipped with a bulldozer blade or not. And when you hear of "bulldozers" in action on the fighting fronts, the chances are they're "Caterpillar" Diesel Tractors.

In addition, sturdy "Caterpillar" Diesel Motor Graders are building military roads and airports around the world. "Caterpillar" Diesel Engines and Electric Sets are powering shovels, crushers, compressors and hoists, generating current for lights, radio and refrigeration, serving as standby power on naval and cargo ships. And "Caterpillar" Diesel Marine Engines drive tugs and smaller war craft.

Workpower is on the side of victory.

CATERPILLAR TRACTOR CO., PEORIA, ILLINOIS

CATERPILLAR
REG. U.S. PAT. OFF.

DIESEL

TO WIN THE WAR: WORK—
FIGHT—BUY MORE WAR BONDS

On both sides of the Atlantic and in military posts around the world, people shared a common experience. "So much of life is being lived anonymously, far from home," wrote Margaret Mead in her essay for *While You Were Gone.* "The soldier or sailor, in a camp or port, far away overseas, has experienced this anonymity over and over again." No wonder so many advertisements centered on the morale of the home-front workers, urging them to "keep their chins up" and to believe that punching the time clock at the factory was much like squeezing the trigger of a machine gun.

One way in which most Americans got to contribute was by paying increasingly stiff income taxes. Walt Disney, whose studios would tackle dozens of war-related projects, produced a film called *The New Spirit* for the Treasury Department. Scholar Richard Shale called it the "most widely seen, as well as the most controversial" of Disney's wartime films. It starred Donald Duck and aimed to educate the nation's 7 million new taxpayers.

A humorous ad from Schenley Distillers Corporation took a more adult approach. It showed an extremely cheerful-looking fellow sitting at his desk at home. He is holding an envelope addressed to Collector of Internal Revenue, has his spectacles pushed up, and is grinning back over his shoulder at the reader. "Worth it!" the headline announces. "Sure, taxes are high—but they buy the tools of Victory—and you can drink to that in a glass of the best—Schenley!" It is a remarkably prescient ad; even today, fifty years later, many taxpayers would heartily agree that a stiff snort sometimes helps.

The 1941 annual report from General Foods Corporation noted, "to win the war, every individual and every organization must make real sacrifices. Your management is in sympathy with the policy of paying for the costs of national protection as we go along." The report said that the company's total US taxes in 1940 had been $6.6 million; in 1942, the taxes increased to $14 million. The Treasury Department, in advertisements, argued that drinking moonshine whiskey was unpatriotic because it "robbed the government of revenues needed for tanks and planes."

The best antidote to confusion and worry at home was to keep busy, which people did, encouraged by ads and posters. As Arthur Upham Pope, chairman of the Committee for National Morale, wrote in the book *America Organizes to Win the War,* "Work itself is a great morale builder. Spirits rarely flag when people are busy, especially when they feel that their busyness

---

We, who are **not** about to die . . .

The homefront cast of characters takes center stage in this November 1943 ad from Parke, Davis & Company, which made pharmaceuticals, biological products, and surgical dressings during the war. The ad exhorted, "Keep on backing the attack—buy war bonds!" at the bottom of the page, noting that the ad was "in behalf of the Treasury's War Bond Campaign."

There's young Bill down the street. He tried to enlist. But he couldn't get past the eye test—even squinting.

There's friendly Jim on the swing shift at the bomber plant who hasn't heard from his son for a long while now.

And Miss Lottie, teacher in the seventh grade, who puts in long hours at the ration board.

And old Hugh, who lost two sons on Bataan—and came to work the morning he got the telegram, same as he'd done for thirty years.

There's the conductor on the 8:14 . . . and the clerk in the grocery store . . . who donate blood as often as they can.

And the stenographers at the office, always busy on something for the boys in camps and overseas.

And there's you—and me

No, we're not risking our lives in this war—but there is a job for us to do.

It's the job of buying the tanks, ships, planes and medicines—all the things needed to win this war, keep our men healthy, and bring them home again. And we can do this by buying War Bonds.

We can take the dimes and dollars that are in the bank or underneath the mattress. The 10% or more of our salaries every payday. The money that might have bought a car or radio.

We can do without the things we're used to having, the things we used to think we needed. And get a kick out of doing it!

We can take the money it almost hurts to give, and put it into War Bonds. For it's those bonds that make us part of what our boys are doing on the fighting fronts. It's those bonds that put us right up almost in the front lines—fighting for a free and decent world.

Until that job is done—well, there isn't much that's *worth* spending money on.

"...AND THERE, 10,000 FEET BELOW

...A BIG 🔻 JAP SHIP!"

"...so we opened up and let 'er have it...a 500-pounder just abaft the funnel." ► "And then what, Uncle Jim?" ► "Then, Billy, old-timer, her fighter escort swarmed in like flies around the sugar...so we streaked it for home...topped the palm trees and set our wheels on the runway, smooth as oil." ► Billy might be amazed to know that hydraulic devices to make bomber wheels come down for safe landings—as well as mechanisms to open the bays through which the big bombs drop—are being made, now, by the same folks who made his mother's Maytag washer.

WE AT MAYTAG are in this war up to our ears—making hydraulic equipment for combat aircraft, among other things. We know our part is just a fraction—but we hope, a vital fraction—of the total effort to bring this war to a quick, victorious end. Then we'll draw a long breath, and . . . *Maytag will be making washers again!* In the meantime, let your Maytag dealer help you keep your present washer in good working order . . . he has genuine Maytag parts when needed.

Fred Maytag 2nd

Maytag

WASHERS   IRONERS

Maytag copywriters deserve a medal for economy in this October 1943 scenario: four sentences, two war-related products. This company's first war-related orders were tank track pins, which they began delivering in June 1941, eventually producing millions of them. Maytag also began making shell adapters, machine shafts, pinions, worms and gears for gyroscopes, castings for bomber and fighter engines, and thousands of electric retraction units for B-17s and B-29s. In all, the company made parts of 16 combat aircraft. From a total of $200,000 in war production in 1941, the company's total exceeded $15 million in 1944. Courtesy, Maytag Co.

is helpful, even essential, to victory." The folks who didn't get jobs in war industries volunteered. By the summer of 1942, 10 million people had volunteered in programs run by the Office of Civil Defense. They worked as air-raid wardens; salvaged rubber, metal, and paper; and sold war bonds.

The May 1942 issue of *Cheesekraft*, a Kraft newsletter, contained a pep talk for employees from the vice president and general sales manager: "Forget the items we don't have—and concentrate on the ones we do have. Stop complaining—and get busy! Get busier than you've ever been before in your life—and stay busy for the duration and much longer."

In the case of conservation drives, these volunteer efforts intersected what was certainly the war's major effect on the American consumer: rationing of some products and a complete absence of others. In some cases, it was a case of less variety. Where shoppers had found five brands before the war, they now found only one. In other cases, high-quality goods were replaced with shoddier substitutes. And in some cases, famous brands and entire categories of goods simply disappeared entirely.

Washing machines were a good example. "When war production reached full swing, 97 percent of the products were for the war, the balance was of washing machine repair parts made in a small section of the plant set aside for that purpose," said the Maytag company history *Yesterday, Today and Tomorrow*. "In this way the many owners of Maytag washers were enabled to keep in operation during the war."

In any case, the war demanded nothing less than a revolution in the habits and preferences of American shoppers, and commercial advertisements led the way with advice, warnings, and pep talks. An ad for the Electric Battery Storage Company cautioned, "If the way you buy gives comfort to the Axis, it's time to call a halt! Buy only what you must."

Before the grand spectacle of war advertising could begin, however, marketing specialists, advertisers, and government officials had to wrestle with the question of whether advertising was necessary at all. They could take some guidance from our British ally across the Atlantic, where the same question had been debated and settled. In *Keep Mum! Advertising Goes to War*, George Begley wrote that the war in England worried British ad agencies. "They foresaw a period in which manufacturers could sell more than they could possibly produce without any advertising at all. Sure enough, food, sweets and clothing were soon to be rationed. Almost everything that was not rationed would be in short supply. In such a situation, how could it pay to advertise?" he asked.

The answer was "brand recognition." British advertising continued apace, as companies and agencies figured out new tactics and developed new messages. "Suppliers of commercial goods . . . poured out hundreds of advertisements, of which the gist was 'Let us remind you that we still exist, but for heaven's sake, don't try to buy our goods'," Begley wrote. Official government ads, coordinated by the Ministry of Information, contained recipes and information about rationing, told readers "how not to get killed in the blackout," encouraged them to mail early, to take part in salvage campaigns, or to enlist.

"The Ministry of Food . . . commanded a demanding position in press advertising during the war," Begley pointed out via a column called "Food Facts," a source of non-stop recipes (one group, for dried eggs, included Curried Hard-Boiled Eggs, Toad-in-the-Hole, Castles in Spain, and Chocolate Cookies). "They'll swear you used fresh new-laid eggs," the copy said, which Begley calls a "courageous but unlikely story." The bottom of

this ad read, "You are allowed one packet of dried eggs per ration book every four weeks." The column's slogan was "Food is a munition of war, don't waste it."

Without exception, these genres of British ads were recreated in the United States. Shortages regularly figured into advertisements, in the form of alternative products, as the theme of conservation drives, or in explanations of why the product was missing from the shelves of the neighborhood market. A classic example is an ad for Campbell's soup, which gave the consumer guidance about how to "make nourishing meals out of war-shortened menus." Even the incentives offered by the ads changed dramatically. Norge Appliance Com-

Another illustration from a wartime Caterpillar ad. The sign on Old Faithful charts American success in battle. According to Caterpillar, "Track-type tractors repaired shelled roads and built new ones, keeping vital supply lines open. They bulldozed tank traps, and built new ones to stop counterat- *tacks. They constructed pillboxes and artillery positions." In the Pacific island-hopping campaign, the vehicles built shallow-water approaches for landing craft, pushed barges off sandbars, and cleared landing strips. Courtesy, Caterpillar, Inc.*

Dairy companies produced a variety of canned dairy products (including cheese, butter, and margarine) for the armed forces, as well as this tropical butter. In 1942, the Kraft plants in Green Bay, Wisconsin, Freeport, Illinois, and Decatur, Indiana, won the first army-navy "E" award for "excellence in production in the food industry" for developing this preserved product. This ad appeared in March 1943. The July 26, 1943, newsletter of N. W. Ayer & Son (the advertising firm that created this ad) reported that this ad drew letters from eight women claiming that they were the mother of the marine in the picture, as well as letters from scores of other relatives. "Not one guessed right!" the newsletter declared, pointing out that in all their ads, "we have used men from that particular branch of the service, and have not relied upon professional models." Courtesy, Kraft General Foods, Inc.

Singapore and Java fell to the Japanese within three months of Pearl Harbor, and the United States promptly lost more than 90 percent of its supply of crude rubber. B.F.Goodrich had produced small amounts of synthetic rubber in early 1939, but the war added intense incentive. By January 1942, the company was making 2,500 tons a year. During the war, the company produced rubber life rafts and pontoons, used by army engineers to make bridges. It also did research on tubeless, self-sealing tires for combat vehicles, so that gunfire couldn't knock the vehicles out of action by puncturing tires. The company also made expander tube brakes for bombers and cargo planes. Courtesy, The BFGoodrich Co.

pany once told the reader, "Keep your war bonds in the free budget portfolio" available from the company.

Americans encountered other shortages in their own driveways. In September 1941, gas and oil distribution on the East Coast was cut 10 percent. Throughout the war, the continuing shortages of gasoline and tires were fertile sources of advertising copy and stories. The General Foods Corporation 1943 annual report showed an employee examining a field of corn. "Even in these days of gas and tire rationing," the caption said, "Harold W. Slocum's essential job requires that he drive 40,000 miles a year. He covers several states . . . contracting for and supervising the growing and harvest of beets, peas, beans, tomatoes, sweet corn and other crops for quick-freezing and canning."

An ad from the United States Rubber Company in September 1942 dramatized the shortage of rubber. It showed Dad, Mom, and Junior striding purposefully forward, with bare feet. "We'll walk barefoot in America if necessary to save rubber . . . to win this war," the headline read. The ad included "Nine Rules for Patriotic Drivers."

BFGoodrich showed the familiar trio with the addition of Grandpa and the family pooch, all (except the dog) thumbing a ride by the roadside. "It's the

Next page
In ads, war and peace blended in a barrage of symbols: farms, industry, ships, aircraft. Note the conservation-minded travel tips. Riding the bus helped save rubber, the reader learned in September 1942. Used with permission of Greyhound Lines, Inc.

KEEPING PACE
with the giant strides of war-time travel

—requires every bus Greyhound can muster . . . every modern means of conserving *rubber, fuel, vital materials!*

How you can help *yourself* and *your country* when taking war-time trips:

- Travel on Tuesdays, Wednesdays, Thursdays—leaving week-ends for men in uniform and war workers.
- Take as little baggage as possible.
- Get trip information from Greyhound agent, well in advance.
- Be at bus stop or station early.
- Don't take unnecessary trips.
- ★ Going Greyhound, it's good to know you're using only a fraction as much rubber per mile as in driving your own car.

Never in history has a war so urgently required so much of transportation . . . never has transportation responded so efficiently. Prime reason for this effective response is that, today, *the highways have taken a huge and important share of the war transportation load.*

Greyhound, carrying millions more passengers than ever in the past, is extending its facilities to the utmost, eliminating all unnecessary services, so that every essential traveler shall reach his destination promptly, without waste of precious time and money.

There are few new buses to be had—there is great need

for conservation—so every coach, every scrap of rubber and metal, every gallon of fuel must stretch farther and farther in service to men in uniform, war workers, farmers and all who must travel to help win this war.

Greyhound could not have successfully carried the capacity loads of the past midsummer season without the fine cooperation of several million travelers—*good sports and good Americans. Our sincere thanks to every one of you!* The biggest part of the job is still to come—and we are confident that, together, we will keep these buses working full-time for Victory.

GREYHOUND

tons of aluminum pots and pans would build bombers or fighter aircraft. The WPB's Salvage Division ran a "Tin to Win" program aimed at recycling a million tons of tin cans a year. Dog food in tin cans had already disappeared from the marketplace, spurring the popularity of dried food. The Campbell Soup Company, Heinz, and Hormel all felt shortages of tinplate for cans and began producing dehydrated foods. In anticipation of a tin shortage, Maxwell House began packing part of its coffee in glass jars in July 1941. To preserve aluminum for combat aircraft, North American built 2,970 plywood AT–6C trainer aircraft, at its Dallas, Texas, plant. Movie theaters offered "aluminum matinees," where the price of admission was an old pot or pan.

Volunteers collected 70,000 tons of scrap aluminum; meanwhile, aircraft manufacturers had discov-

ered that they could use only virgin aluminum. Scrap dealers bought the salvaged stuff and turned it back into pots and pans.

In April 1942, if you wanted to buy toothpaste, you had to turn in the empty tube. Cellophane vanished at one point. The scarcity of gas and tires meant that most grocery stores stopped deliveries; they were delighted to find out that shoppers spent about 20 percent more when they came in person. However, for the shoppers, just getting to the store was sometimes a struggle.

The number of people who rode buses doubled between 1941 and 1944 and, as a result, bus service was described as both "erratic" and "overcrowded." Gasoline shortages were sometimes severe enough to curtail or limit the routes. All modes of transportation were strained to the limit. In *Women at War with America* D'Ann Campbell tells the story of one hapless lad whose "father took his tire swing for the automobile, mother commandeered his wagon for groceries, brother took his skates to help with his paper route, and older sister borrowed his bike to ride to her new job at the shipyard."

In late 1942, shortages of leather goods (particularly, shoes), stockings, kitchen utensils, and toys were

The Dixie Cup Company was originally incorporated as the American Water Supply Company of New England in April 1908. The company vended drinks of water and other beverages. The founders quickly perceived that paper cups were sanitary and helped safeguard public health; at that time, the public shared a common cup or dipper at public fountains. The company helped develop a portable water tank for the armed forces in 1941. "World War II settled for all time the question of the value of paper cups and containers to public health and public service," a company history said. The inset column in this December 1942 ad shows that Dixie Cups were "on many fronts," including bombers, arsenals, and factory cafeterias. Courtesy, James River Corp.

Early in the war, when the threat of air raids hung heavy over the American coasts, adults signed up as volunteer wardens. Meanwhile, kids had a new hobby: junior air warden. The aircraft in this illustration suggests a B–24.

apparent. Supplies of elastic thread, metal buttons, zippers, hooks and eyes, canvas and duck, and some types of leather, were cut off, those materials going directly into war-related goods. Facial tissue and toilet paper almost disappeared.

Shortages affected consumers and companies, alike. In May 1942, for example, the Florida Citrus Commission noted some of its problems: "... the inclusion of canned citrus in the Maximum Price Regulation which guaranteed producers minimum price levels when maximum prices were set upon their products. Another immediate problem was the looming shortage of wires and nails for citrus containers." In January 1943, a shortage of wood compelled citrus packers to experiment with fiberboard.

Ray-O-Vac couldn't use metal for flashflights, so the company switched to plastic (which became hard to get), and then to paper and molded fiber.

Colgate-Palmolive needed fats, oils, and rosin to make soap, using coconut oils from the Philippines, palm oil from Sumatra and Africa, and olive oil from the Mediterranean. Most of the sources of supply were eliminated early in the war. In 1942, the use of fats and oils in civilian soaps was restricted to 84 percent of the amount used in 1940–41 and was further reduced to 80 percent in July 1943. Shortages and rationing of shipping containers, tin, glycerine, alcohol, paper, and essential oils also affected the company's production.

According to the 1943 annual report from General Foods, "Maintenance of plant equipment became increasingly difficult. Few new machines were obtainable, repair parts were scarce or not to be had.... Only the ingenuity of plant personnel and the cooperation of thousands of employees kept GF's processing and packing lines moving throughout the year with a minimum of mechanical and human failure." Armstrong's production was hampered by shortages of cork, rubber, zinc oxide, burlap and linseed oil (both essential to linoleum), asphalt, and tinplate.

Federal agencies made sweeping decisions about the jobs and products deemed "essential" to the war. Sometimes the reasons behind those decisions weren't obvious. The Dixie Cup Company was "established as an essential industry, and it wasn't long before Dixie cups and containers were being delivered on a priority basis, first to the armed forces, of course," a company history said. "After we had supplied the demands of public service organizations like the Red Cross, hospitals, etc., of war industries for in-plant feeding, of ice cream manufacturers who had orders for the deliveries of ice cream Dixies or Pac-Kups to Army camps and schools, we could sell to our civilian customers." All Dixie products were stringently rationed, in part because of paper shortages.

Shoes were rationed at two pairs per year, about half the normal consumption. A Florsheim Shoe Company ad in August 1942 tried to make people feel better about the leather shortage: "America will march to victory on the leather you save," it said. Alternative

footwear was also scarce. In *Since You Went Away* Donald Rogers recalled, "Those who owned sneakers cherished them highly, for there was no such thing as rubber-soled shoes."

It would be simple-minded to think that every single American cheerfully accepted all of the rationing and shortages. The war served as a great rumor mill, since credible information was often as scarce as some tangible products. In 1942, for example, "The shortages of meat, sugar, fuel oil and gasoline were attributed to bungling rather than genuine shortages ... there was also a sour conviction that Americans were going without all kinds of scarce and desirable things so that the British and the Russians would not have to," Geoffrey Perrett wrote in his book *Days of Sadness, Years of Triumph*. Complainers and rumor-mongers were

Humor was rare in wartime posters, articles, and ads, but unhappy consumers were common. Armstrong Cork Company produced this poster in January 1944 to take some of the sting out of shortages. Courtesy, Armstrong World Industries, Inc.

among the typical cast of villains of wartime ads, as were people who bought or sold things on the black market.

An ad for Seagram's Five Crown liquor contained this pertinent verse:

*"A black market cheat
has got to be beat!
Appoint yourself a special cop
And help your country put a stop
To underhanded dealing. . . .
The guy who flouts the O.P.A.
Is injuring us all, today
So why not crack his ceiling!"*

The ad contains a little "Buy War Bonds" poster on the wall in the drawing. The ad is unusual because, as a rule, advertisements for liquor studiously avoided mentioning the war.

Historians agree that black markets were sporadic and isolated, however. "Only a handful of people even condoned the black markets which mushroomed in the last year of the war," Perrett wrote. "Most people who bought black market goods did so unwittingly."

Sugar shortages would continue for the duration of the war. In its 1944 annual report, General Foods noted

All metals were in short supply during the war. In this ad from February 1943, Bell Telephone explains that, instead of going into telephone wires, copper is being used to make bullets. In a similar 1942 ad, entitled "He's firing telephone wire at a Zero!", the copy said, "This fighter plane, with its six wing guns spitting fire, uses up enough copper every minute to make several miles of telephone line."

the difficulty it had had trying to get enough sugar to produce such familiar products as Jell-O desserts and Log Cabin syrups. In 1944, it was permitted to use only 80 percent of the sugar it had used in 1941, a ration that was quickly reduced to 70 percent.

Throughout the war, advertisers tried to explain shortages to consumers, usually in the jargon of the times. A 1944 ad for Snider's condiments was entitled, "We put a Victory Garden in every bottle!" Snider's catsup and chili sauce, the ad said, were "just what you need to liven up wartime menus. But remember, folks—if you have a little trouble now and then getting any of our Snider Sauces, it's because we're shipping lots of good Snider vittles to the armed forces these days."

On Father's Day in 1944, many potential gifts were not available in stores: shoes, tires, lawn mowers, cigarettes, leather belts or wallets, golf balls, radios, bristle brushes, fountain pens, camping equipment, or boxed candy. You could buy cigars and neckties. Earlier in the war, on October 5, 1942, *Life* magazine had featured an illustrated list of suggested Christmas gifts for "men overseas," based on polls of what the soldiers and sailors wanted. The list included many items that would be in short supply later in the war: portable radios, waterproof wrist watches, cigarettes (the magazine illustration showed the Camel brand), small cameras, homemade jelly, slippers, and family photos. Perhaps the soldiers and sailors got their gifts while the getting was good.

The ideal wartime consumer appeared in a 1944 ad from the National Dairy Products Corporation. She was a veritable war-effort dynamo, and the ad may have set a record for the number of different wartime themes introduced. It pictured a mother and son on a bike with carrier basket full of food. "Marketing was certainly simpler in the car. . . . oops, there goes a potato! . . . but it's a lot easier to park a bike—and cheaper, too. . . . hold on, Johnny, we're coming to a corner!" Mom said. "An American sense of humor has helped Mrs. Frazier make the best of food, gas and rubber rationing," the ad copy continued. "It's rather fun balancing a big box of groceries in front and a small boy in back. It's not so much fun balancing coupon points against the high prices, and low stocks in the stores. But there's still a certain satisfaction in being clever enough to make things come out even! . . . In the same cheerful, chin-up spirit, she has pitched into the other wartime jobs. Little things bother her most—the lack of elastic, bobby pins, zippers. But she's doing all her own cleaning since once-a-week Mary went to work at the plane plant. She's saving fats, flattening cans, baling paper. She grows vegetables instead of flowers in the backyard. . . ."

It would have taken the government five pamphlets and three posters to cover all that ground. During the war, advertising writers and designers were just like Mrs. Frazier, balancing topics and themes. Usually, they, too, did it cleverly and cheerfully.

Make way

War's on the wires

Army, Navy and war industry *must* have quick communication.

It takes a lot of telephone calls to move a million men or make munitions — 12,000 calls for example, to make a bomber.

As the war effort speeds up, the load on telephone wires grows. We can't build new lines to carry it because copper, nickel and rubber are shooting, not talking, materials right now.

But what we can do is make the most of what we have. You can help if you will not make any Long Distance calls unless they are really necessary. Even on these, please be as brief as you can.

The call you save today may speed a plane or tank to the fighting front.

WAR CALLS
COME FIRST

BELL TELEPHONE SYSTEM

The Bell Telephone System issued a series of simple, striking ads. Unlike today, when telephone ads urge you to make more calls, during the war the message was to cut down. It would be interesting to know how someone figured out that it took 12,000 phone calls to make a bomber. This ad appeared in September 1942. Another Bell project involved air-raid sirens, in chronic short supply until the summer of 1942, when the Office of Civil Defense and Bell Laboratories brought out a "Victory" model, so powerful that "it could rupture eardrums at a hundred paces," one historian said. Courtesy, AT&T Bell Laboratories

UP WHERE MAN HAS NEVER
FOUGHT BEFORE

NASH-BUILT ENGINES WILL BLAZE A ROAD TO VICTORY

In the new battle-field of the sky—where war was never waged before—it's a freezing 50° below zero, and air is one-fifth of its sea-level density. Ordinary engines would starve and die.

Yet into these shuddering heights a plane is lifting—soaring up like a rocket. Through his oxygen mask, the pilot is confidently smiling—and the mighty song of the engine never falters.

It's the U. S. Navy's *Corsair*—a ship designed to outclimb, overtake and outfight any known Nazi or Jap in the sky!

Its secret—a mighty 2,000 horsepower Pratt and Whitney engine, super-charged a new way for high-altitude combat—an engine that will be built in quantity by the men of Nash and Kelvinator.

Look again in the far-flung reaches of the sky—

Soon there will be full fleets of great, four-engine flying boats bearing large numbers of fighting men and gigantic loads of matériel for the U. S. Navy! These cargo carriers will be built by Nash-Kelvinator.

Look farther—thousands of planes of many types are already flying to battle fronts of the world on propellers made by Nash-Kelvinator.

This is our job—and we are *in it to win*—with all the strength and skill and production genius we can muster.

And when that great day finally comes—when the last Nazi swastika is shot out of the sky—then you will find that from the crucible of war the men of Nash and Kelvinator have brought new skill into building the automobiles and refrigerators for America at peace.

NASH-KELVINATOR CORPORATION

NASH KELVINATOR

PRATT & WHITNEY HIGH-ALTITUDE ENGINES

NAVY'S GIANT VOUGHT-SIKORSKY FLYING BOATS

HAMILTON STANDARD PROPELLERS

Chapter 2

The War Production Board

"The Reminders Of The War Were Everywhere"

"Here's what we're doing for the war effort!" was the dominant theme of wartime advertising. While American consumers were finding less variety and fewer products in the stores, there was no shortage of ads, and the government was on a $300 billion spending spree.

The companies that placed the ads had reasons for being self-congratulatory about their contributions to the military, especially compared to the starting point. In 1940, when half of the world (measured by population and land area) was at war, the US Army was smaller than that of either Greece or Poland and one-tenth the size of the German army.

Most people didn't seem to want to go to war, and the government agencies charged with military preparation and national defense bitterly debated whether to gear up for an offensive in Europe or to prepare for the coastal defense of North America. As a result, our efforts were weak and scattered. After Pearl Harbor, the Fourth Air Force (which was tasked with defending California) had a pitiful total of 34 bombers and 113 interceptors. West Coast aviation squadrons could launch a grand total of only 45 modern fighter planes.

Problems with military equipment were common. Although the M-1 rifle had been adopted in 1936, a much greater number of Springfield Model 1903 rifles were still around. Plenty of surplus material and gear from World War I was still in military supply systems.

The topic of rearmament was in the public spotlight, but it was not unanimously supported. As early as 1939, companies such as Armstrong Cork Company had set up War Activities Committees. In 1940, Armstrong accepted an "educational contract" to make 5,000 75-mm high-explosive shells. Also in that year, the Association of American Railroads produced 690,000 copies of the booklet *Railroads and the*

Previous page
The copy for this ad shows Nash-Kelvinator s hard-boiled writers at their best. They deserved an award for tough, punchy copy. Courtesy, White Consolidated Industries, Inc.

Although specific war work made up just 22 percent of the production of Armstrong Cork Company (today, Armstrong World Industries) from 1941 to 1945, the output was still impressive. The company made 4 million brass and steel cartridge cases, 45 million square yards of concealment material, and nearly 11 million magnesium bombs. Armstrong also made nearly 3 million bomb racks for aircraft, more than 60 million navy projectiles, and 27,000 plastic canopies for aircraft. It made wingtips for navy PBM-3s, and fins and rudders for Corsairs. It fireproofed and waterproofed material for tents and tarpaulins and made felt covers for anti-tank mines. The total of munitions orders was $111 million. Other civilian products went heavily to the military as well: building materials, glass, closures, and linoleum. Courtesy, Armstrong World Industries, Inc.

45

National Defense and a quarter-million copies of other pamphlets about "railroad capacity and preparedness."

American industry also produced military equipment for the British. In April 1938, the British Purchasing Commission had come to the United States with a budget of $25 million to spend. Lockheed showed them a Model 14 converted to a medium reconnaissance bomber. In June, the Air Ministry placed an order for 200 of them, plus as many more as could be delivered by December 1939, up to 250. "It was the largest single order ever received by any American aircraft manufacturer," a company history said. The British called the aircraft the Hudson, and Lockheed would build nearly 3,000 of them by May 1943, delivering nearly 2,000 to the British Royal Air Force (RAF). In September 1939, a Hudson became the first RAF airplane operating from the United Kingdom to shoot down an enemy airplane in World War II.

Woe to its foe!

Over scorched desert sands and far at sea—swift, formidable Grumman "Martlets" are helping the British Fleet Air Arm add inspiring chapters to its illustrious record. These reliable carrier-borne and land-based fighters are designed and built to "take it" and "dish it out," as the foe well knows.

Grumman Aircraft Engineering Corporation
Bethpage • Long Island • New York

American manufacturers got crucial experience before Pearl Harbor by making aircraft, tanks, and weapons for America's allies-to-be. On Christmas 1941, above the Orkney Islands, three British F4F Martlets intercepted a German Ju 88 bomber, and one of the Martlets shot it down. It was the first kill for an American-built fighter during the war. Courtesy, Grumman History Center, Grumman Corp.

In April 1940, North American started making AT-6 Harvard trainers for the British and French. Also, Douglas Aircraft was making A-20 Bostons, and Lockheed was making P-40 Tomahawks. In late 1939 and early 1940, the British had also asked North American to make P-40s. The company offered to design a better fighter, the NA-73 (which was later designated the P-51), and the British Purchasing Commission agreed in April 1940 to buy 320 of them, renaming it the Mustang I. The first P-51s used Allison engines, which made what company historian Bill Yenne described as "a surprisingly reliable and capable airplane, but not a great airplane," in the book *Rockwell—The Heritage of North American*. The RAF came up with the idea to retrofit it with a Rolls-Royce Merlin engine (which Packard was making in the United States), turning it into a superior performer. This version was called the P-51B; North American would make nearly 2,000 of them.

The legislative key to this help was the Lend-Lease Act in 1941, HB 1776, "A Bill to Further Promote the Defense of the United States, and for Other Purposes," which formalized the process that was already at work. It was an extraordinary law, wrote Geoffrey Perrett in *Days of Sadness, Years of Triumph*. "In a document only several pages long 'any' appeared thirty-five times. Regardless of any existing legislation to the contrary, the President could at any time take anything he wished and put it to any purpose he deemed important to the nation's security." The WPB would exercise similar powers later in the war and, in both cases, willingly or unwillingly, both consumers and businesses would feel the results.

Many other companies produced goods for Lend-Lease. For example, Caterpillar made track-type tractors, motor graders, and generator sets.

Yet, these educational contracts and production runs were small and tentative. Many historians detect a general, subtle reluctance on the part of big business to convert to war industries, even after Pearl Harbor. There were a number of valid reasons for this hesitation: doubt that postwar markets would exist, the feeling that jobs would be scarce after the war, or the chance that the war would end unexpectedly.

"Roosevelt's main problem—really the nation's main problem—was to create a war economy in a nation still formally at peace," Perrett wrote. "The solution he settled for, however reluctantly, was to rely on

Next page
In February 1940, the British contracted with Lockheed for a military version of the Model 18 Lodestar, to be called the Vega Ventura, eventually ordering some 700 of them. At the end of 1942, all Venturas went to the US Navy, which got 1,600 of them and called them PV-1s. In April 1941, Vega also joined with Boeing and Douglas to make B-17 Flying Fortresses, which, along with the B-24, was the core of the AAF's daylight bombing campaigns in Europe. Vega made 2,750 B-17s. Courtesy, Lockheed Corp.

WHAT DO YOU MEAN

medium
bomber!

There's nothing "medium" about our American
medium bombers but their size. For example, the
Vega Ventura can bomb accurately from high-level
flight—swoop down on its target for low fast attack—
strafe troop concentrations—blast tanks—tow gliders
loaded with men and supplies, and tow high speed
targets for our fighters to practice on—a combination
of tasks no other medium bomber can do.

Then, too, the Ventura patrols thousands of miles of
cold gray ocean to drop depth charges when it finds
a sub—carries torpedoes to attack enemy ships—
plants mines to trap them. What do you mean,
"medium" bomber!

The Ventura has the same basic qualities of *all* Lockheed and Vega planes, *extra* strength, *extra* dependability. That's why the Canadian, British, Australian,
and U. S. Army and Navy Air Forces are all using
Venturas—lots of them.

A subsidiary of Lockheed

Vega

Aircraft Corporation

Lockheed Hudson
Medium Bomber

Lockheed P-38
Lightning Fighter

big business. And by the fall of 1941 big business had done so badly that there was no longer any way of hiding it."

"The insistence of many companies upon 'business as usual' was an obstacle to all-out war production," Alvin Dodd wrote in his 1942 book, *America Organizes to Win the War*. "In the early stages of the defense program it was mistakenly believed that industry could take arms production in stride and could supply the nation with both guns and butter. As the war went on, however, it became apparent that business could not go on as usual."

On May 14, 1940, five weeks before France fell, Congress authorized a build-up of 4,500 planes, and upped the ante to 10,000 on the next day. Unfortunately, authorization and hardware are two different

Wheels Turning and Fires Burning

In his annual message to Congress on Jan. 6, 1942, President Roosevelt sketched a dizzying increase in military production as a response to the Japanese attack on Pearl Harbor and the American declaration of war. The urgency expressed in this statement would become one of his hallmarks during the war and a national attitude, as well.

Victory requires the actual weapons of war and the means of transporting them to a dozen points of combat.

It will not be sufficient for us and the other United Nations to produce a slightly superior supply of munitions to that of Germany, Japan, Italy, and the stolen industries in the countries which they have overrun.

The superiority of the United Nations in munitions and ships must be overwhelming—so overwhelming that the Axis nations can never hope to catch up with it. In order to attain this overwhelming superiority the United States must build planes and tanks and guns and ships to the utmost limit of our national capacity. We have the ability and capacity to produce arms not only for our own forces but also for the armies, navies, and air forces fighting on our side. . . .

This production of ours in the United States must be raised far above its present levels, even though it will mean the dislocation of the lives and occupations of millions of our own people. We must raise our sights all along the production line. Let no man say it cannot be done. It must be done—and we have undertaken to do it.

I have just sent a letter of directive to the appropriate departments and agencies of our Government, ordering that immediate steps be taken:

1. To increase our production rate of airplanes so rapidly that in this year, 1942, we shall produce 60,000 planes, 10,000 more than the goal set a year and a half ago. This includes 45,000 combat planes—bombers, dive bombers, pursuit planes. The rate of increase will be continued, so that next year, 1943, we shall produce 125,000 airplanes, including 100,000 combat planes.

2. To increase our production rate of tanks so rapidly that in this year, 1942, we shall produce 45,000 tanks; and to continue that increase so that next year, 1943, we shall produce 75,000 tanks.

3. To increase our production rate of anti-aircraft guns so rapidly that in this year, 1942, we shall produce 20,000 of them; and to continue that increase so that next year, 1943, we shall produce 35,000 anti-aircraft guns.

4. To increase our production rate of merchant ships so rapidly that in this year, 1942, we shall build 8,000,000 dead-weight tons as compared with a 1941 production of 1,100,000. We shall continue that increase so that next year, 1943, we shall build 10,000,000 tons.

These figures and similar figures for a multitude of other implements of war will give the Japanese and Nazis a little idea of just what they accomplished in the attack on Pearl Harbor.

Our task is hard—our task is unprecedented—and the time is short. We must strain every existing armament-producing facility to the utmost. We must convert every available plant and tool to war production. That goes all the way from the greatest plants to the smallest—from the huge automobile industry to the village machine shop.

Production for war is based on men and women—the human hands and brains which collectively we call Labor. Our workers stand ready to work long hours; to turn out more in a day's work; to keep the wheels turning and the fires burning twenty-four hours a day, and seven days a week. They realize well that on the speed and efficiency of their work depend the lives of their sons and their brothers on the fighting fronts.

Production for war is based on metals and raw materials—steel, copper, rubber, aluminum, zinc, tin. Greater and greater quantities of them will have to be diverted to war purposes. Civilian use of them will have to be cut further and still further, and, in many cases, completely eliminated.

War costs money. So far, we have hardly even begun to pay for it. We have devoted only 15 per cent of our national income to national defense. As will appear in my Budget Message tomorrow, our war program for the coming fiscal year will cost fifty-six billion dollars or, in other words, more than one-half of the estimated annual national income. This means taxes and bonds and bonds and taxes. It means cutting luxuries and other non-essentials. In a word, it means an "all-out" war by individual effort and family effort in a united country.

Only this all-out scale of production will hasten the ultimate all-out victory. Speed will count. Lost ground can always be regained—lost time never. Speed will save lives; speed will save this Nation which is in peril; speed will save our freedom and civilization—and slowness has never been an American characteristic.

Yank pilots nicknamed it "Invader"

During the fierce battles for Sicily and Italy, a brilliantly engineered new plane speeded our victory.

Officially known as the A-36, the new North American fighter-bomber was adapted from the famous P-51 Mustang. An American correspondent, reporting on this sensational new ship, cabled:

"The scream of this plane when it dives would shake any man. It makes a Stuka sound like an alley cat.

"When it levels off at the bottom, and lays those bombs right on the target, it zooms away as a heavily-gunned fighter, looking for Axis troops to strafe, for enemy planes or tanks or trains to destroy. It's a hot ship...plenty fast and plenty rugged. No wonder our jubilant pilots nicknamed it 'Invader.'"

But perhaps more important than its destructive power is the way the Mustang saves lives...the lives of *our* soldiers.

Blast the enemy's planes out of the air ...disrupt his communications...devastate his supply depots and transportation...destroy his offensive power... and you make the task of our ground forces infinitely easier, safer. With air superiority, it's as simple as that.

Through constantly improved designs, and field service on every fighting front, the men and women of North American Aviation are enabled to set the pace in an industry which safeguards America's future. The more and better planes they build, the sooner Axis resistance will be smashed...and the more American lives will be spared.

North American Aviation, Inc., designers and builders of the B-25 Mitchell bomber, AT-6 Texan trainer and the P-51 Mustang fighter (A-36 fighter-bomber). Member of Aircraft War Production Council, Inc.

North American Aviation *Sets the Pace!*

49

Previous page
North American's masterpiece was the P-51. Reichsmarschall Herman Goering admitted that he realized they'd lost the war when P-51s appeared over Berlin. Nearly half the enemy aircraft shot down over Europe were claimed by Mustangs. There were 5,595 Mustangs in AAF inventory at the end of June 1945. Courtesy, Rockwell International Corp.

things. Federal planners talked of a $100 billion defense effort in 1941, but only half that had been appropriated by the fall of that year and less than $20 billion contracted for. Only $7 billion was spent by the end of the year, and problems persisted. In January 1942, official predictions about shortages in military material were grim. Of the thirty-five army divisions, only ten would have all their equipment three months later; the others would have about half. To make matters worse, three or four new divisions were being formed every month.

Once the shooting started, everyone needed more stuff and more quickly than anyone thought possible.

War documentary figures into this July 1943 ad, which points out the illustration (showing Western ammo on Guadalcanal) was based on "an actual photograph released through the War Department." Courtesy, Olin Corp.

The United States had virtually no munitions industry, for example, yet a single division required 162 Browning automatic rifles, fifty-four .30–caliber light machine guns, seventy-two .30–caliber heavy machine guns, thirty-six .50–caliber machine guns, eighty-one 60–mm mortars, thirty-six 81–mm mortars, and thirty-six 37–mm anti-tank guns.

In *America Organizes to Win the War*, Alvin Dodd (president of the American Management Association) asked, "What did we need? Principally these things: airplanes, airplane engines, heavy guns, light guns, trench mortars, tanks, shells, machine guns, automatic rifles, regular rifles, rifle ammunition, fighting ships, merchant ships, camps and cantonments, airplane factories, tank factories, smokeless-powder factories, trucks, shell-loading factories."

In the year after Roosevelt's "Arsenal of Democracy" speech, the percentage of the country's productivity going into defense tripled. The growth went this way: On July 1, 1940, America was spending $165 million per month on defense. That figure reached $500 million per month on January 1, 1941, $900 million per month in July, and $2 billion per month in December 1941. When the Japanese attacked Pearl Harbor, the military had grown from 189,000 men two years earlier to 1,450,000 men.

Military planners found it easier to enlist soldiers than to equip them. In the factories, myriad production problems remained. The British had been fighting the Luftwaffe and knew what aircraft they needed. American industry was making fifty-five kinds of planes. Propellers, landing gear, tires, bombs, and bomb releases weren't standardized, which interfered with mass production. These problems—foggy planning, scarce materials, uncoordinated production—were only a few of the gigantic challenges facing American industry after Pearl Harbor.

Since it took 90,000 worker-hours to build a four-engine bomber, it was a small wonder that everyone seemed to be in a hurry. "Every job is a fighting man's job," declared a 1942 poster from the Sheldon-Claire Company of Chicago. "Minutes count with freedom at stake. Let's cram them full of work! Produce for victory!" The solution to the challenge wasn't just a matter of hiring, hurrying, and spending, of course. Numerous

Next page
North American was another of the great names in aviation, rightfully blowing its own horn in this ad. The company began building the BT-9 Yale trainer for the army in 1935. Another of the company's trainers, the AT-6 Texan and Harvard, was indispensable in the huge expansion of the AAF, helping train the pilots who would in turn fly the fighters and bombers. "The AT-6 was the airplane of the hour, the keystone of what would become the biggest air force the world would ever see," company historian Bill Yenne wrote. From 1934 to 1967, North American (and its later incarnation, Rockwell) built more military aircraft than any other company, including 41,000 during World War II. Courtesy, Rockwell International Corp.

51

Night Patrol

"WE were flying routine night patrol," said the bomber pilot, in relating the incident which won for him a letter of commendation from the Commanding General. "Flying at 1000 feet, we saw the sub surface. Descending to 300 feet and flying at 300 miles per hour, we switched on our landing lights; and as we passed over the sub, bracketed it with four depth charges."

In accordance with Army regulations, names are omitted in this story from COMMAND POST, McClellan Field, Calif.

This is the G-E Airplane landing lamp—*generally used for safer landings, but employed by this pilot to help blast a sub. Built in the same way as your G-E Sealed Beam headlamps, it is only one of over 200 lamps used on the average big bomber.*

When the last patrol has flown and the lights come on again, General Electric Research will be seeking new ways to bring you brighter, happier living. Health-giving ultra-violet . . . fluorescent "daylight" for kitchen or bedroom . . . and other new applications of light. Right now so many G-E lamps are serving our fighting forces that it is important to make the most of the lamp bulbs you have. Keep your G-E Mazda lamps clean, keep them close when you read or work, and turn them off when not in use. Conserve for Victory!

To make lamps STAY BRIGHTER LONGER
THE CREED OF G-E RESEARCH

G-E MAZDA LAMPS
G-E MAZDA LAMPS

G-E MAZDA LAMPS

GENERAL ⊕ ELECTRIC

Hear the General Electric radio programs: "The G-E All-Girl Orchestra", Sunday 10 p. m. EWT, NBC; "The World Today" news, every weekday 6:45 p. m. EWT, CBS.

BUY BONDS FOR VICTORY

ICE CUBES FOR JAPAN !

Listen, Tojo—when you hear that *kar-rump* some night and the factory walls start sliding into the sea—look out, it's one of those new "ice cubes" from Nash-Kelvinator!

We are building *plenty* of them just for you—huge Kelvinators that fly and ice cubes that hurt.

Monster metal-bellied flying boats—growing on Nash-Kelvinator assembly lines—to whisk the Navy's men and material to any spot you raise your head! Giant Vought-Sikorsky cargo carriers built *complete*—and not in ones or twos, but in fleet upon fleet!

Want to hear some more?

Then listen—that angry hum coming out of the East—

They are the propellers built by Nash-Kelvinator, built by the many thousands!

And that mighty roar you'll soon be hearing is the voice of the most powerful engine ever placed in a pursuit ship. It will take the Navy's new *Corsair* higher, faster than any "Zero" in your stable.

They're coming, Tojo—coming from men who, in building last year's refrigerators and automobiles, thought only of a nation's health and happiness.

But now, it's hate and vengeance and the remembrance of a thousand Axis wrongs that are guiding their hands . . . beating every production record in Nash-Kelvinator history by two and three.

Look out, Tojo, *the nights are growing longer.*   .   .   .

NASH-KELVINATOR CORPORATION

NASH KELVINATOR

This slogan plays on Kelvinator's better-known role as a maker of refrigerators. The Kelvinator Company had its roots back in 1914 in a company called The Electro-Automatic Refrigerating Company, which made the first household mechanical refrigerators. The later company was named in honor of Lord Kelvin, the British physicist, and the company was acquired by Nash Motors in 1937. During the war, Nash-Kelvinator made Vought-Sikorsky cargo planes and Pratt & Whitney engines for the navy's Vought Corsairs and Grumman Hellcats. The company also made bomber propellers, governors, binoculars, and parts for ships, tanks, and trucks. Courtesy, White Consolidated Industries, Inc.

In 1944, Oldsmobile hired women to replace men in such jobs as forging and machining; before the war, women had worked primarily in inspecting and assembling. The company called them Wings, shorthand for War Working Women of Oldsmobile, and gave them uniforms, caps, and a winged patch (worn by the woman in this photo). Courtesy, Oldsmobile History Center

needs of both the military and the civilian economy, the WPB determined what manufacturers would make, thereby virtually decreeing what shoppers would find when they went to the store. Both of these things were clearly reflected in wartime ads; companies had a lot of explaining to do.

It was only logical that President Roosevelt would look to industry when choosing a chairman of the WPB. He tapped Donald Nelson, who described himself as "chief merchandising executive of the world's largest distribution firm," in his book *Arsenal of Democracy*. Nelson had been with Sears, Roebuck and Company for thirty years and had risen to the rank of executive vice president. Since Sears dealt with 5,000 manufacturers in the United States and owned (wholly or partly) twenty-five manufacturing businesses, Nelson was an inspired choice.

"Nelson Gets World's Biggest Single Job," trumpeted a *Life* headline in January of 1942, calling him "the No. 1 figure of the war effort." The magazine's biography of Nelson said that "If the U.S. population had been sifted to find the one man who best and most completely represented the way of life for which the war is being fought, Nelson would have been an almost ideal choice."

The WPB geared up quickly; one unit, which dealt with textile, began as part of the Office of Production Management in March 1941 with two people. By early 1942, it had 300, and soon had 500. This ballooning staff mirrors the growth of the federal government itself,

which grew from one million employees in 1940 to nearly four million on VE Day.

Nelson chose as a member of his personal staff David Noyes, a partner in the advertising agency of Lord and Thomas and Logan, which was the second largest such firm in the country in the late 1920s. Nelson wrote that Noyes had a "keen and dependable insight into the psychology of the public." Other influential figures from American industry also went to Washington. The president of General Electric, Charles E. Wilson, was the number two man in the WPB. Sherrod Skinner, head of Oldsmobile, went to the WPB in August 1942 for a six-month stint as director of the Production Division.

The WPB quickly made its influence felt by people across the country. One of its first orders gave

Next page
Western Electric produced a series of at least 16 of these well-illustrated scenes during the war, featuring many theaters of war and combat specialties, as well as one of the company's products. This installment appeared in May 1944.

Page 58
Another edition of the Western Electric series illustrated by Paul Rabut. This one appeared in July 1945, as the war entered its final stages.

Every branch of the Armed Services uses the telephone. No. 11 of a series, Infantry.

Battle Talk! . . . that is what he handles on this portable switchboard. Close behind our advancing troops, he holds the life lines of men in combat. Through these lines, flow reports from outposts, orders from command posts—helping to win objective after objective on the road to Victory, Home and Peace.

What can he do with your money?

He and his comrades can win this war with it—when you turn your dollars into weapons. The cost of winning is high—but dare you think of the cost of NOT winning? Make sure of Victory—invest every dollar you can in *War Bonds!*

75TH ANNIVERSARY
Western Electric

IN PEACE . . . SOURCE OF SUPPLY FOR THE BELL SYSTEM
IN WAR . . . ARSENAL OF COMMUNICATIONS EQUIPMENT

57

Traffic Cop of Invasion — that's the Navy Beachmaster! He comes ashore with one of the first waves of fighters to direct the landing of troops, weapons and supplies. One of his crew "broadcasts" his commands over a powerful loudspeaker. Keeping order in the midst of seeming chaos, he speeds the taking of another stepping stone to Victory.

Until the war is won, Western Electric will continue to supply vast quantities of "battle talk" equipment to our armed forces. Then — and only then — can we return fully to our primary job of producing equipment for the Bell Telephone System.

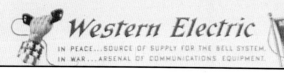

Western Electric

IN PEACE...SOURCE OF SUPPLY FOR THE BELL SYSTEM.
IN WAR...ARSENAL OF COMMUNICATIONS EQUIPMENT.

You've got a part in his job!

He works for days at a stretch getting guns, tanks, ammunition, gasoline, food, medical stores and countless other supplies ashore. Our fighters must have more and more of these things. Buy more War Bonds — and keep all you buy!

End of an Enemy

THIS enemy plane is headed for doom. In a split second it will be blasted from the skies by a shell from one of our anti-aircraft guns on the ground.

How can a gun hit a plane going 300 miles an hour 20,000 feet up . . . when it takes the shell 15 seconds to get up there and in that time the plane has gone more than a mile? Besides, the shell curves in its flight. Wind blows it. Gravity pulls on it. Even the weather affects its velocity.

The answer is the Gun Director—an *electrical* brain which aims the guns. Swiftly it plots the plane's height and course. Instantly it solves the complex mathematical problem, continuously matching the curved path of the shell to the path of the

plane so that the two will meet. It even times the fuse to explode the shell at the exact instant.

The *electrical* Gun Director has greatly increased the deadliness of anti-aircraft gunfire. Developed by Bell Telephone Laboratories and made by Western Electric, it is one of many war weapons by the peacetime makers of Bell Telephones.

Until the last enemy plane is knocked down,
buy War Bonds regularly—all you can!

Western Electric
IN PEACE...SOURCE OF SUPPLY FOR THE BELL SYSTEM.
IN WAR...ARSENAL OF COMMUNICATIONS EQUIPMENT.

The artist, Anton Otto Fischer, produced several well-known posters during the war for the Office of War Information, including "A Careless Word . . . A Needless Loss" in 1943 (a response to the successes of German U-boats early in the war) and "A Careless Word . . . A Needless Sinking" in 1942. Fischer was an official artist for the Coast Guard, working for the Coast Guard's Graphic Unit in White Plains, New York. This ad appeared in February 1944.

members of the military priority at airports. For a civilian who wasn't traveling on war business, taking the train wasn't a very helpful option, either. The railroads were already jammed; they moved 600,000 troops during the sixteen days after Pearl Harbor.

The WPB often squabbled with the military over who would control war production and the importance of the civilian economy. After Pearl Harbor, Nelson recalled, the military "adopted what was to be their policy for the duration: astronomical quantities of everything and to hell with civilian needs."

This in-fighting produced numerous spates of inflammatory headlines. In his memoir of the war, Donald Nelson accused the army of manipulating the press: "That barrage of 'scare' publicity, guaranteed to appeal to the fears and the patriotism of readers in every section of the country, was the sort of thing the army could and did turn on whenever it wished to do so."

The heat produced by errors in planning or priority, Nelson came to learn, usually made itself felt at his desk first. A minor but revealing example occurred in July 1942. The WPB ordered a halt in production of civilian alarm clocks because the metal used to make them was needed elsewhere. By the following spring, war plant managers were complaining because so many of their workers were arriving at work late. As a result, WPB approved a "victory model" clock made from a minimum amount of metal.

The transformation of industry was innovative, rapid, and sometimes surprising. To some businesses,

the war meant salvation. Companies that had made wooden frames for automobiles had been slowly dying since automakers started to switch to steel bodies in the 1930s. These companies easily and gladly shifted to assembling wooden gliders for the army. In Massachusetts, it was a cinch for the General Crib and Cradle Company to start making cots. Other changes were less obvious: A company that canned citrus fruit made parts for ships. A grower of ferns made bomb chutes. Companies that made machinery for processing cotton

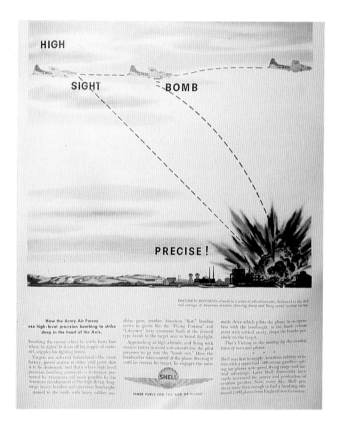

This February 1944 ad from Shell falls into the category of the combat-tactics lesson. Here, the reader receives a somewhat optimistic version of precision bombing. Shell's major role in war production was making 100-octane gasoline, which was "one of the important production stories of the war," wrote Kendall Beaton in Enterprise in Oil—A History of Shell in the United States. Shell had shipped small quantities of "commercial iso-octane" to the Air Corps at Wright Field in April 1934. Shell foresaw its important future in aviation, in part thanks to Jimmy Doolittle, who was then aviation manager of the American branch of the company. Compared to 75-octane fuel, 100-octane increased power in existing engines by 15 to 30 percent. In January 1938, the army recommended 100-octane fuel for combat and that all Air Corps engines be designed to use it. The American combat forces would use some 20 million gallons during World War II. Shell made about 13 percent of that total. During the war, Shell also produced butadiene (a critical component of synthetic rubber), made a synthetic toluene (needed in TNT), and invented a process for purifying penicillin. Courtesy, Shell Oil Co.

In April 1941, Oldsmobile began producing 20-mm aircraft cannon. The company assembled the cannon, but made just 3 of the 132 parts—the barrel, bolt, and receiver—and 58 outside suppliers made the rest. On August 21, 1942, Oldsmobile workers finally got a close look at the tank for which they'd been building 75-mm cannons. The Sherman tank was in Lansing, Michigan, for an army program called Salute to Agriculture, Industry and Labor. Similar programs brought homefront workers closer to the battle fronts. Courtesy, Oldsmobile History Center

On the *World's Fastest "Tricycles"*

this clever tube insures safer landings

MANY of America's fastest new fighters and bombers are equipped with a tricycle landing gear, built with a full-sized wheel under the nose. It permits pilots to fly these "hot" ships in with tails up and land at speeds once thought impossible. But to avoid crack-ups it is essential that the airplane be protected against the dangers of nosewheel deflation.

This is accomplished by a clever Goodyear development known as the Dual-Seal inner tube, embodying the same principle

as the famous Goodyear LifeGuard. This tube has two air compartments. It is so constructed that, if the casing and outer tube are punctured, *the inner section expands and fills out the tire to normal size.* Even if the puncture occurs on the take-off, this double tube retains enough pressure to insure a safe, smooth-rolling landing after a long flight.

Today the Dual-Seal tube is protecting American airplanes and pilots, operating all over the world on makeshift

desert and jungle fields. Before Pearl Harbor, tricycle landing gear was in prospect on our commercial air transports, too. Now this must wait until victory comes. But Goodyear will be ready for these great new airliners of a better world—ready with airplane tires, tubes, wheels and brakes brought to new perfection in the crucible of war.

HOW THE DUAL-SEAL TUBE PREVENTS PUNCTURE CRACK-UPS

If a thorn, cactus spike or jagged rock punctures casing and outer tube compartment, inner section expands, rounding out tire to full normal size as in No. 2. It holds enough pressure to keep tire firmly seated on rim and maintains sufficient rolling radius to assure a safe landing.

LifeGuard—T. M. The Goodyear Tire & Rubber Company

Making tire tubes was one of Goodyear's minor tasks during World War II; the company also designed and made wheels, tires, and brakes. It produced gas masks, ailerons, and flaps for B-26s, and 200,000 rubber boats, life rafts, and pontoons. Goodyear made more than 4,000 Corsair fighter planes for the navy, and turned out a million bullets a day at another factory. It also cooperated with other companies in making complete wings and tail surfaces for the Martin B-26. Courtesy, Goodyear Archives

I am the boots of a fighting paratrooper, specially built to give my guy the best "jumping boots" in any man's army. When my trooper bails out to do battle, it's "curtains" for some enemy-held position. To do his job well, and live to fight again, my soldier depends on you for the chutes and planes and weapons you buy for him — with your War Bonds. Keep him in there fighting — buy another Bond today.

JARMAN-BUILT FOR "SOLDIERS IN CIVVIES"

Like the paratroop boots and "GI" shoes Jarman makes for our fighting men, this Jarman "Million-Aire" style is designed for essential service — especially built to give comfort and long wear to you men who serve America here at home in "civvies."

The special buoyant insole and distinctive *friendliness* of fit give you real, lasting walking comfort — like walking on a deep, soft carpet wherever you go.

Just *try* on a Jarman "Million-Aire."

Best buy for your ration coupon at $5.85 to $8.85 most styles

Jarman
SHOES FOR MEN

JARMAN SHOE COMPANY · DIVISION GENERAL SHOE CORP. · NASHVILLE, TENN.

One of Jarman's *"Million-Aires"* with the patented cushion insole from heel to toe. This is Style No. 2108, see it at your Jarman dealer's.

JUST TRY ON A PAIR OF JARMANS — LET THE SHOE HORN BE THE JUDGE

64

"Service men who reported that they spent hours in replacing a seal on the old type said they performed the same service on a Maytag unit without removing it from the plane and completed the job in not to exceed forty-five minutes," a company history said. "Maytag men and women know that when they read of raids made by these bombers that it was they, figuratively speaking, who were reaching out to . . . open or close the bomb bay doors through which bombs were dropped on enemy targets."

Historian Geoffrey Perrett emphasized that workers such as these would prove to be the crucial factor. "The key to defense production was not, in the final analysis, either the vastly overrated 'know-how' of businessmen or the state of labor-management relations," he wrote. "America would outproduce the world in arms because it already possessed the physical and psychological tools: a large, skilled, disciplined population, mechanically minded, well fed and energetic, occupying a land rich in natural resources and possessed of a capital investment, accumulated over decades, worth hundreds of billions of dollars."

Conversion of the automobile industry was the first major item on the WPB agenda, and merits its own chapter in this book. It had 500,000 employees scattered through 1,300 cities, and more than 1,000 factories. In the few weeks after Pearl Harbor, the auto industry took war orders of $14 billion, and the rate at which demands increased was mind-boggling. In 1941, between the time Buick had agreed to make Pratt & Whitney engines and had found a place to build the new plant required, the government had raised its contract from 500 engines a month to 1,000, then 3,000, then 4,400. All told, the auto industry would fill 10 percent of all war production.

Donald Nelson felt that Hitler was "convinced that cutthroat competition among American manufacturers under the free-enterprise system would prevent them from getting together, pooling their resources, sharing their equipment and trade secrets, and operating as a team soon enough to disturb his timetable."

Of course, some competitive pressure was relieved by the fact that the war produced more than enough business for almost everybody. Plants and factories began to compete for production records. The commercial aircraft industry, among the most competitive of all, showed tremendous unity, Nelson recalled. "Commercial rivalries vanished in the smoke of war," he wrote, "and the industry emerged as a vast system of aircraft production that dwarfed anything on earth."

From 1935 to 1939, Grumman had been building about forty fighters per year for the navy. Its production of fighters quickly climbed to forty a month. In 1939, American industry had produced 5,865 planes, mostly civilian types, amounting to 6.6 million pounds of airframes. It produced 83.5 million pounds of airframes in 1941, 276 million in 1942, and 667 million in 1943. In 1944, aircraft plants turned out 96,369 aircraft, including 9,117 in March of that year alone.

Non-industrial companies had undergone similarly explosive expansions, both in terms of how much they produced and where that output went. The 1941 annual report of the National Dairy Products Corporation announced that the government had greatly increased production goals for the following year, demanding 900 million pounds of cheese, 3.5 billion pounds of evaporated milk, and 525 million pounds of dried skim milk. Like ads, annual reports stressed the importance

Next page
The Glenn L. Martin Company was an early entrant in the race to increase war production. In 1939 and early 1940, the company supplied 115 Model 167 attack bombers to France and thereafter to the British. Martin Mariners saw service in the north Atlantic and in the Pacific. The B-26 Marauder, accepted by the army in 1939 as the standard medium bomber, first rolled off the assembly lines in November 1940. The B-26 would turn up as a torpedo bomber at the Battle of Midway, but most of the 5,500 B-26s saw action in the European and Mediterranean theaters, forming the backbone of the 9th and 15th air forces. On D-day, Marauders spearheaded the invasion forces. Martin built some 1,500 B-26s at its government-built plant near Omaha, Nebraska, shifting over to making B-29s there until the end of the war. One of those planes dropped the first atomic bomb. Courtesy, Martin Marietta Corp.

The Axis knows these Aircraft well . . . do You?

1 Mighty Middleweight, this lightning-fast, heavily-armed medium bomber is pounding the Japs from the Aleutians to the Solomons . . . blasting the Nazis in Europe. Recognize her stubby wings, torpedo-shaped fuselage, all-plastic nose? *See answer at lower left.*

2 Plenty of Punch is packed into this big 24-ton, twin-engined Navy flying boat. Easily recognized by its gull wings and up-tilted tail assembly, this patrol bomber has done excellent work in the Atlantic and elsewhere. Can you name her? *See answer at lower left.*

3 Fast Freight reaches fighting fronts quickly in this long-range, two-engine Navy transport. Big sister of plane No. 2 above, she has the same general silhouette but weighs four tons more and lacks gun-turrets. Could you spot this plane? *See answer at lower left.*

4 Built for Britain by a famous American company, this twin-engined, low-wing bomber won laurels in desert warfare over North Africa. Extremely fast, she carries a crew of 3, has sufficient firepower to serve as a long-range fighter. Know her? *See answer at lower left.*

You won't recognize this Airplane

. . . because it hasn't yet been built. And it won't look like this, either. But 125-ton airliners of advanced and unusual design will be familiar sights, after Victory. Already complete on Martin drawing boards, such mighty ships need only peace to become reality. After the war you'll be able to circle the globe on a two weeks' vacation with ample stopovers for sightseeing. That's why we say, buy War Bonds today . . . because you're going places, tomorrow!

THE GLENN L. MARTIN COMPANY, BALTIMORE, MARYLAND, U.S.A.
THE GLENN L. MARTIN COMPANY—NEBRASKA COMPANY—OMAHA

The Martin Planes pictured above are:

1 "MARAUDER"
   Army Bomber

2 "MARINER"
   Navy Patrol

3 PBM-3
   Navy Transport

4 "BALTIMORE"
   British Bomber

Martin
AIRCRAFT

Builders of Dependable Aircraft Since 1909

"I JUST HEARD SOMETHING WE CAN TALK ABOUT!"

★

It's no secret that, plane for plane, American warplanes can outfly and outfight the Nazis and the Japs. That's because the engines of all American warplanes are designed for high-octane gasoline.

Everybody also knows, or should know, that only the United States has plenty of all the *three* things needed to produce large quantities of high-octane gasoline: 1. Vast resources of fine crude oils. 2. Superior refining processes, developed by the American petroleum industry. 3. Adequate production of anti-knock fluid to increase octane ratings of military gasolines.

The makers of Ethyl brand of anti-knock fluid have geared their plants, laboratories and technical staffs to meet the oil industry's war need for anti-knock fluid. Our Army, Navy and Allies will have plenty of Ethyl for fighting fuels. And that's no secret!

ETHYL BRAND OF ANTI-KNOCK FLUID IS MADE BY THE ETHYL CORPORATION

AMERICA'S
VAST RESOURCES OF HIGH
QUALITY CRUDE OIL

+

SUPERIOR REFINING
PROCESSES DEVELOPED BY
OUR PETROLEUM INDUSTRY

+

ADEQUATE PRODUCTION
OF ANTI-KNOCK FLUID
(containing tetraethyl lead)

=

Superior Fighting Fuels

67

Previous page
Ethyl Corporation figures prominently in the history of American chemistry. In 1921, the company's future founder (Charles Kettering) and his staff (working for the General Motors Research Corporation) invented tetraethyl lead as a practical anti-knock compound for internal combustion engines, vastly increasing horsepower in automobile and aircraft engines. Kettering once quoted the British as telling him "if it had not been for tetraethyl lead they would have lost the Battle of Britain." Plants were producing the anti-knock fluid in Germany (1936), France (1938), and England (1940), and the Nazis built an unauthorized plant in 1939. A Nazi sub fired on the Ethyl-Dow plant in North Carolina on July 25, 1943, testimony to the enemy's view of the product's importance. The worker in this Ethyl Corporation ad is indicating an example of one of the distinctive genres of wartime posters: the loose-lips-sink-ships group. The ad appeared in May 1942. Note the typical exhortatory banner at top center. Reprinted with permission of Ethyl Corp.

Light aircraft were among the forgotten workhorses of the war, serving as a sort of airborne jeep in artillery spotting and liaison duties. This one flies over a Sherman tank; note the hand signals. The last dogfight of the European war featured one of these aircraft and a German counterpart, the pilots using pistols, in April 1945. This ad also highlights the work of Walt Disney, who, in addition to designing hundreds of insignia for aviation squadrons, made instructional films for Beechcraft, Aeronca, and Minneapolis-Honeywell, and cartoon mascots for Aeronca (Abel Grasshopper) and Beechcraft (a bee). Courtesy, Aeronca Aircraft Co.

of the company's contribution: "Foods as well as planes and tanks are vital, for the effectiveness of armed forces depends to a great extent upon good nutrition. In 'total war,' moreover, the health and morale of every civilian worker play an extremely important part in the drive for victory," the report said.

The growth of the armed forces matched that of industry's production. In 1939, the army had 167,000 men. At the end of 1941, it had ten times that, and by the end of 1944, the total was 8.3 million. The AAF grew from 354,000 men in 1942 to 2,385,000 in 1944.

A 1942 WPB poster showed President Roosevelt at the base of a V, out of which rises a dense stream of aircraft in an upward V-shape (this "endless stream" motif appears in several wartime ads). "In 1942 America will build 60,000 war planes," the poster caption said. "In 1943 America will build 125,000 war planes."

"These totals were so vast that Axis propagandists promptly scoffed at them," Donald Nelson wrote, "but like other 'impossible' jobs, this one got done—with something to spare, too."

After the tide of battle turned in favor of the Allies, homefront planners had to keep workers from relaxing their efforts. In an article called "The High Cost of Victory" in the December 1943 issue of *Reader's Digest*, Nelson stoked the production fire. He pointed out that one thousand aircraft workers had to work forty-hour weeks for a year to replace the sixty bombers lost in one day in the Schweinfurt raid, and that even though the 105–mm howitzer can be fired 7,500 times before the barrel wears out, "We wore out hundreds of them in Sicily in 30 days," he wrote. "Victories call for more and more material, not less."

Federal press releases and most advertisements painted a hunky-dory picture of wartime production, but reality wasn't quite so flawless. The WPB was charged with favoring big industries over small businesses, and (in the case of electric power) favoring private industry over government-owned sources of power. And there was no denying that the war had devastated many of the nation's two million small-business owners. Auto dealers and washing-machine distributors were the types of businesses hardest hit.

The WPB record wasn't quite as unblemished as it appears in Nelson's memoirs. By April 1942, it was clear that (as in 1941) some of the WPB goals wouldn't be met. Instead of $60 billion worth of war construction and production, it looked like $50 billion and would turn out to be $44 billion.

Next page
Sixteen B–25s were used in the Doolittle raid on Tokyo in April 1942, mentioned in this ad from May 1944. Some 1,600 B–25 variants (the G and H models) had the 75–mm nose cannons, also mentioned in this ad, which were the largest guns ever put in a US combat aircraft. Nearly 10,000 Mitchells were made during the war, and only 380 were lost in combat. Courtesy, Rockwell International Corp.

15-gun salute from American flyers

There's "no future" for Japs and Nazis who tangle with the crushing firepower of the 15 guns packed by the new B-25 Mitchell bomber. Today's Mitchell—6000 design improvements more deadly than the model in which General Doolittle bombed Tokyo—bristles with heavy armament. From the 75-mm. cannon in its nose to the "stingers" in its tail, the Mitchell's guns blast the enemy on land and sea, protect its five-man crew against air attack. As they shoot to win on eleven fronts of this global war, the victorious B-25s are helping mightily to soften up the enemy, to make the job of American fighting men all over the world easier, safer.

North American B-25 Mitchell

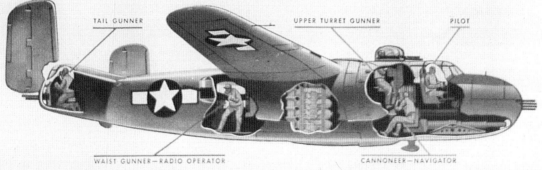

TAIL GUNNER UPPER TURRET GUNNER PILOT

WAIST GUNNER—RADIO OPERATOR CANNONEER—NAVIGATOR

FIREPOWER PLUS MANPOWER! The B-25 Mitchell and its 5-man crew fight together as the world's hardest-hitting medium bomber team!

North American Aviation Sets the Pace

In spite of these sporadic black eyes, during the war, business was good. In 1943, corporate earnings topped those of the previous record year, 1929. A survey of eighty-eight contractors found that only two had rates of annual profit below 6 percent, and about half were earning 40 percent. Overall, business profits were up about 20 percent. Corporate assets climbed from $54 billion in 1939 to $100 billion in 1945.

To many people, there was something unseemly about the idea of making profits as a result of America's campaign to make the world safe for democracy.

The top of this photo shows part of Grumman's F6F Hellcat assembly line. Grumman started delivering Hellcats in September 1942, and delivered 12,275 through November 1945. At bottom, an employee needs a ladder to reach the top of the delivery chart; the charts to the left are for the TBF Avenger and F4F Wildcat, and are plotted to the same scale. "Future increases will require a higher ceiling and obviously a taller girl," the photo's original caption said. Grumman set a national production record for aircraft in March 1945: 605 Hellcats and 59 airplanes of four other types, an average of 22 aircraft per day. In 1942, the navy asked for extra Wildcats to back the Marine invasion at Guadalcanal, and the company responded by hitting a peak production rate of fifteen a day, compared to the usual three. During the war, Grumman produced almost a billion dollars' worth of military aircraft. Courtesy, Grumman History Center, Grumman Corp.

According to Allan Nevins, "Unquestionably there was a general feeling by 1944–45 that big business and union labor were taking more than their proper share from the common pot."

If you surveyed the headlines and opinion polls from the war years, you would find them to be typically American, full of fiery rebukes, jarring opinions, and conflicting interpretations. After the war ended, Stalin toasted American war production, "without which our victory would have been impossible." And without which, the comfortable retrospective criticism of the pieces of the equation wouldn't have been possible.

Before Pearl Harbor, one fact had been clear to Donald Nelson and to countless other war planners and workers. Once America entered the war, the country would "be engaged in a struggle without a limit, a struggle conducted strictly on a winner-take-all basis," Nelson wrote in his book about the war years. "It would be a struggle in which all of our strength would be needed—and the penalty for being unable to use all of our strength would be the loss of everything we had. No matter what the obstacles in our way, we simply had to be thinking in terms of doing our utmost."

Although wartime advertisements were only transitory reflections of the greater currents at work in society, they clearly showed that everyone was thinking in exactly those terms.

Next page
North American had been making the B-25 for four years when this ad appeared in February 1944. The twin-engine medium bomber was first flown in August 1940. The company made the first delivery of 24 that September. Mitchells would pay their dues around the combat globe, flying from airstrips in Pacific jungles, North African deserts, and Alaskan tundra. The AAF, navy, and RAF all flew B-25s. North American began the production run of the B-25C, of which it would make 1,625, in January 1942. Courtesy, Rockwell International Corp.

Page 72
Before America entered the war, the Anglo-French Purchasing Commission ordered 667 P-38s (the RAF had called it the Lightning), but only three were ever delivered. The AAF received all production starting in December 1941. Lockheed made more than 10,000 P-38s in 18 versions. The P-38 was the first American plane to shoot down an enemy plane after the United States declared war: a Lightning knocked down a Focke-Wulf Condor patrol bomber near Iceland. From Pearl Harbor to VJ Day, Lockheed built a total of 19,297 aircraft, 9 percent of all US production. Courtesy, Lockheed Corp.

Page 73
In February 1943, Bell Aircraft blended journalism and advertising in a typically wartime way, mixing an Associated Press clipping with hard-boiled prose and a classic headline. Courtesy, Bell Aerospace Textron

ZERO ÷ B·25 = 💥

Tojo's boy's are learning simple arithmetic from Uncle Sam's...

Typical is this flyer's report:

"Newspaper stories of American flyers knocking down Jap planes by the dozens, while losing only a few, are absolutely correct. I remember the gunner of my B-25... as soon as the Japs got within range of his .50 caliber machine gun, he began firing bursts to keep the Jap away. He protected our ship very well, and when there was a Jap pilot with guts enough to come in close,

the gunner made it so hot for him that the guy sheered off. This gunner got three Zeros.

"Another time, our B-25's and fighter escort were jumped by 40 or 50 Zeros. We got 23 for sure, probably 9 more, and lost one plane. The ratio of Jap losses to ours is really high!"

That's just a pilot's way of saying that Zero divided by B-25 equals zero—and always will!

The men and women of North American Aviation are delighted to have a hand in the education of the Sons of Heaven... proud to supply, as the lethal divisor in this simple

problem in American arithmetic, the B-25 Billy Mitchell bomber—"the old reliable," flyers call it.

North American Aviation planes, brilliantly engineered and soundly built, have had no small share in the outstanding achievements of American flyers on every front of this global war.

North American Aviation, Inc., designers and builders of the B-25 Mitchell bomber, the AT-6 Texan combat trainer and the P-51 Mustang fighter (A-36 fighter-bomber). Member of the Aircraft War Production Council, Inc.

North American Aviation *Sets the Pace!*

71

Tough Customer

Concentrated firepower... a smashing blast of machine gun bullets and cannon shells spitting from one point—and heading hell-bent for the target.

That's the kind of firepower that makes a warplane a tough customer. That's the kind of firepower a Lockheed P-38 "Lightning" has...concentrated firepower that's designed in—not added on.

And it's firepower that is *always* concentrated...from muzzles to target, at any range...because it comes slamming from the nose of that unobstructed center cockpit. It's a battle-axe of lead and explosives that can slice off a Messerschmitt wing, or blast a Jap Zero to bits...and it's another reason why a 'plane christened "Interceptor Pursuit" in defense-minded days fits so well its new official air force title, "Fighter"! Lockheed Aircraft Corporation...Vega Aircraft Corporation...Burbank, California

for protection today, and
progress tomorrow, look to

Lockheed

FOR LEADERSHIP

ALL FIRST CLASS MAIL *by* AIR

IT'S COMING!

Member Aircraft War Production Council, Inc.

72

Tonight's lesson for Japs
...subtracting Zeros

A great guy takes off, and a headline is in the making... a headline about courage and spunk and Army Bell Airacobras that help him shatter Jap Zeros into "kingdom come." From General MacArthur's Headquarters, Australia, October 12th (A.P.) comes news of the citation for "gallantry in action" of this Army Pilot.

Capt. Mainwaring was leading a flight of Airacobras over New Guinea on May 28 when one of his planes was attacked by eighteen Jap fighters. Turning back he shot down the leader of the enemy formation and scattered the others. He then reformed his own group and made a co-ordinated attack, destroying three more and possibly shooting down two others.

Under control of the Airacobra pilot is one of the world's hardest-hitting fastest-moving one man arsenals. Forward is a powerful cannon. Flanking him are heavy machine guns. Around him is protective armor and behind him is an outstanding record of Airacobra success in combat.

The day is coming when Allied Victory will end this war. An advanced world of air-borne commerce will follow. Then, all of our engineering skill and resources will turn from the needs of war to building planes for the needs of Peace. © Bell Aircraft Corporation, Buffalo, New York.

Airacobras for victory—
FUTURE PLANES FOR PEACE

BELL *Aircraft*

PACEMAKER OF AVIATION PROGRESS

"Nice goin' baby!"

First in the automotive industry to fly the Navy "E" with three stars, Fisher has also been awarded the Army-Navy "E" for its ahead-of-schedule tank production.

So it goes, on a dozen fronts — American industry backing up American men with fire-power, with a rising flood of war tools and transport, with a heightening volume of all kinds of ordnance.

The Fisher contribution to this effort, in terms of volume, is huge. But volume alone fails to tell the whole story of the Fisher effort. For the long-acquired skills of the Fisher craftsmen are today playing a part of national importance. They have a vital and specific value of their own.

Our country's leaders realize that it takes precision men to do a job precisely — that extreme standards of mathematical exactness must be met in order to surpass the technical excellence of our enemy's war machines. And Fisher, as a precision center, has been honored with a number of very difficult assignments.

Our fighting men are doing the big job. But the vicious snick of our well-turned breech-blocks, the roar of our tanks, the bark of our anti-aircraft guns are music to their ears.

armament
BODY BY *Fisher*

DIVISION OF GENERAL MOTORS

Chapter 3

Detroit Goes To War

"Minutes Count With Freedom At Stake!"

In the late 1930s, a small number of American military planners and businessmen began playing very serious games of "What if?" What if the war in Europe got bigger? What if the United States got involved? They knew that we were dramatically unprepared, and that modern war would demand massive industrial output. They had to look no farther than the thriving, gigantic American automobile industry to begin planning for contingencies. It had 130,000 machine tools (about half of the country's metalworking capacity) and directly involved one thousand factories in thirty-one states.

The first tangible step was the formation of the Automotive Council for Air Defense in October 1940; it would later become the Automotive Council for War Production. The story is told in detail in *Freedom's Arsenal*, published by the Automobile Manufacturers' Association (AMA) in 1950.

One of the key players was William S. Knudsen, former president of General Motors, who supervised industrial production for a pre-war federal agency called the National Defense Advisory Commission (NDAC). Knudsen was also a former director of the Automobile Manufacturers' Association. At a meeting of the AMA in October 1940, Knudsen confessed "his grave concern about the state of the nation's unpreparedness for the war which was then threatening to engulf the world." Not one to go halfway, he asked the members, as an industry, to supply "a half billion dollars' worth of critically needed airplane parts and subassemblies," items that most of them had never even seen, much less made. Pearl Harbor was more than a

year in the future, and the American public was clearly undecided about participation in the war.

As evidence for this need, Knudsen cited the observations of Gen. Henry "Hap" Arnold, chief of the US Army Air Corps (which became the US Army Air Force on June 20, 1941), who had recently returned from viewing the effects of aerial bombardment in England. Knudsen and Arnold agreed that existing aircraft manufacturing facilities would need to be expanded by a factor of ten to twenty.

The membership of the AMA then included companies that went on to become the giants of the industry for half a century: Chrysler Corporation (which then made Chrysler, DeSoto, Dodge, and Plymouth automobiles); Ford Motor Company (manufacturing Ford, Lincoln, and Mercury automobiles); General Motors Corporation (maker of Buick, Cadillac, Chevrolet, Oldsmobile, and Pontiac automobiles); International Harvester Company; Packard Motor Car Company; Studebaker Corporation; and Willys-Overland Motors, Inc. Among the AMA's two dozen members were oth-

Next page
When Donald Nelson, head of the WPB, wrote his memoir of the war, Arsenal of Democracy, he cited American tank production as one of our specific strengths: "It might almost be said that the Nazis did us a favor when they perfected the tank and its tactical uses, because we, of all nations, were best equipped to convert to tank production and turn out tanks in almost limitless quantity, and of various qualities and kinds." Courtesy, General Motors Corp.

Previous page
The artist, Dean Cornwell, was a muralist and illustrator who also produced war posters, including a well-known war bond poster captioned, "Victory—now you can invest in it." Note the typical wartime adaptation of this company's familiar Body-By-Fisher logo. Courtesy, General Motors Corp.

Page 77
In January 1944, Willys-Overland offered this "true incident from the Battle of the South Pacific," a tale of heroism and violent death. The ad is notable because it recognizes one of the less-glamorous branches of the service, and contains a classic slogan: "The sun never sets on the mighty jeep." Courtesy, Chrysler Corp.

Cadillac

Some go Through – Some go Over !

Under the direction, and with the cooperation, of Army Ordnance—Cadillac has developed, and is building, what have proved to be two of the most effective pieces of armament in the Arsenal of Democracy.

One is the M-5 Light Tank—a fast, quick, highly-maneuverable weapon, armed with a high velocity, 37 mm. cannon. This tough, speedy, hard-hitting tank is one of America's great "surprise weapons"—ideal for upsetting enemy formations. Like a speedy halfback, it darts through the slightest opening in the line,

or "runs the ends," as the need may be. It is almost as fast as a motor car.

The other is the M-8 mounting the Army's 75 mm. Howitzer cannon. Utilizing the same chassis as the M-5, it gives to demolition artillery a degree of mobility it has never known before. With this weapon, big guns can follow their targets—keep the position from which they can do the most good.

The two units that give these weapons their power and maneuverability were developed by Cadillac in peacetime: the Cadillac V-type

engine and the Hydra-Matic transmission.

The quickness with which these peacetime units were sent to war not only attests their inborn quality of design and construction—but it indicates the splendid manner in which Army Ordnance has utilized the nation's resources to astound the world with its armament program.

CADILLAC MOTOR CAR DIVISION  GENERAL MOTORS CORPORATION

76

77

ers that would disappear, including Diamond T Motor Car Company, Hudson Motor Car Company, Hupp Motor Car Corporation, and REO Motors, Incorporated.

What the Automobile Companies Made

An appendix in *Freedom's Arsenal, The Story of the Automotive Council for War Production* lists the wartime production totals of the automobile industry. Statistics are lifeless entities, but the list offers vivid insight into the vast sweep and colossal amounts of material used by America's military. *Freedom's Arsenal* was published by the Automobile Manufacturer's Association in Detroit in 1950.

The following list of products produced by motor vehicle, body, parts and accessories companies, is as comprehensive a tabulation of the automotive industry's production for World War II as has been possible to obtain. Compiled in 1947, it is incomplete because it does not embrace all of the end products made by automobile, body, and parts factories, nor does it take into account the huge volume of components, such as vehicle and aircraft sub-assemblies and parts.

4,131,000 Engines

Aircraft	455,522
Marine	168,776
Tank	257,117
Military Trucks	3,250,000

5,947,000 Guns

Carbines and Rifles	3,388,897
Machine Guns	2,276,204
Anti-Aircraft	156,313
Other Guns	125,527

2,812,000 Tanks and Trucks

Tanks	49,058
Amphibian Tanks	5,115
Gun Carriages (Tank Type)	24,147
Gun Carriages, Other; and Armored Cars	126,839
Military Trucks	2,600,687

27,000 Complete Aircraft

Airplanes	22,160
Helicopters	219
Gliders	4,290

Automotive Industry Percentage of Total War Output

Complete Airplanes	10%
Machine Guns	47%
Carbines	56%
Tanks	57%
Armored Cars	100%
Scout Cars and Carriers	92%
Torpedoes	10%
Land Mines	10%
Marine Mines	3%
Army Helmets	85%
Aircraft Bombs	87%

The auto industry wasn't starting on military production from scratch. The Cadillac Motor Car Division of General Motors had started building inner assemblies (crankshafts, camshafts, connecting rods, supercharger gears, and impellers) for the Allison aircraft engine in March 1939. Later, Cadillac would also produce the M–5 light tank, which was armed with a 37–mm cannon, and the motor carriage for the M–8 howitzer, which was armed with a 75–mm cannon. During Lend-Lease, Packard had taken on the job of translating the British blueprints for the Rolls-Royce Merlin engine for American production, and the Saginaw Steering Gear Division of General Motors had accepted a trial order to make 500 .30–caliber Browning tank-type machine guns in June 1940.

In the summer of 1940, Ford engineers helped develop the final design for the jeep; earlier models had been produced by Willys-Overland and the American Bantam Automobile Company. The experience of the latter company typifies the boom-or-bust currents of the times. The military needed huge amounts of everything immediately, a situation that clearly favored large, established employers. American Bantam had done much of the development work on the jeep, but it was too small and couldn't expand fast enough to meet the government's needs. So, a pair of much larger companies—Ford and Willys—got the contracts to build most of the 634,000 jeeps that were produced by 1945. American Bantam faded from the scene.

At the AMA's seminal meeting in October 1940, the auto makers created a committee for the NDAC to study how they could make the transition from wheels to wings by participating in aircraft production. At this point another famous name in military aviation entered the tale. The US Army Air Corps provided blueprints and drawings, and made Maj. James Doolittle of the Wright Field Material Division available to give technical advice and explanations. If any auto makers were still lukewarm about making the transition, Jimmy Doolittle was just the guy to give them the spark.

In November 1940, the United States committed to making 38,500 planes for American forces, as well as 10,000 more for the British. Furthermore, 102,000 aircraft engines were on order. The federal government agreed to build four new aircraft plants, which would be managed by airplane companies. Two of the sites were Kansas City (to be run by North American Aviation Corporation) and Omaha (to be run by the Glenn L. Martin Company).

On January 4, 1941, President Roosevelt created a new agency, the Office of Production Management (OPM), with Knudsen as chairman. (Knudsen had been commissioner of industrial production in the Office for

Next page
The strikingly executed illustrations and gripping yarns put this series from Willys-Overland in the front rank of the ads that told wartime action narratives. This ad appeared in November 1943. Courtesy, Chrysler Corp.

A salute to the fighting men of the United States Army Ground Forces

HEROIC OFFICERS DARE DEATH FOR MEN

(A true incident of the invasion of North Africa)

THE JEEP has carried brave men into countless thrilling actions on every blazing front of the war. But never has a Jeep participated in a more heroic deed than is described in the incident illustrated above.

Here is the story as told, *for the first time*, by a commanding officer of the United States Ground Forces that landed at Port Lyautey:

"It was very early morning of the day we invaded North Africa, and we were standing off the shore of Casablanca. Directly in front of us lay the resort town of Port Lyautey, one of the strongest fortified points held by the French. It was here that their Commandant had his headquarters in an old Portuguese fort, on a hill five hundred yards in from shore.

"Just at daybreak our barges, manned by Navy personnel, and carrying Jeeps, tanks, and men of the United States Army Ground Forces, took to the water. We headed for shore in surf that was 18 feet high.

"When we were about half way in, they opened up on us with everything they had. Even before we reached the beach, their guns and fliers were making it plenty hot for us.

"Our Jeeps were the first to hit the sand and they came off the barges with their guns blazing.

"Throughout the whole action, the teamwork of the U.S. Army and Navy forces was *perfect*.

"But there was one example of personal courage in those three days of fighting that will stand out in my memory if I live for a thousand years.

The heart of every fighting Jeep in the world—and the source of its amazing power, speed, flexibility, dependability and fuel economy—is the Willys "Go-Devil" Engine, the design of which was perfected and is owned exclusively by Willys-Overland.

"You see, the commanding officer of our expedition—an oldtimer—carried an important message for the Commandant at the fort. He felt that if this message got through, there was a good chance that they would quit firing and that much bloodshed would be prevented.

"So, on a standard to the right of his Jeep he had an American flag set up. On the left, the Tri-color. And in the middle a flag of truce.

"The message had to reach the fort. Our Commander, and another officer who volunteered to drive the Jeep, made the attempt.

"With those three flags standing straight in the breeze, this Jeep came off the barge first. It headed across the beach and on up the hill toward the fort, at top speed— *right into the fire of a battery of 138 mm. coast artillery guns and machine guns.*

"We figured that if the officers in the fort saw their own flag along with the 'truce' flag and the Stars and Stripes, they would cease firing, and the message would get through.

"But it didn't work out that way. When the speeding Jeep was about two-thirds the way up the hill, and we were thinking they might make it, a burst of gun-fire killed the Colonel and knocked the Jeep out of action. The other officer escaped with his life, and although captured, completed the mission, and later received the Congressional Medal of Honor.

"And right there the curtain came down on one of the finest bits of personal heroism, *above and beyond the call of duty*, that this war will see on any front."

WILLYS BUILT JEEP

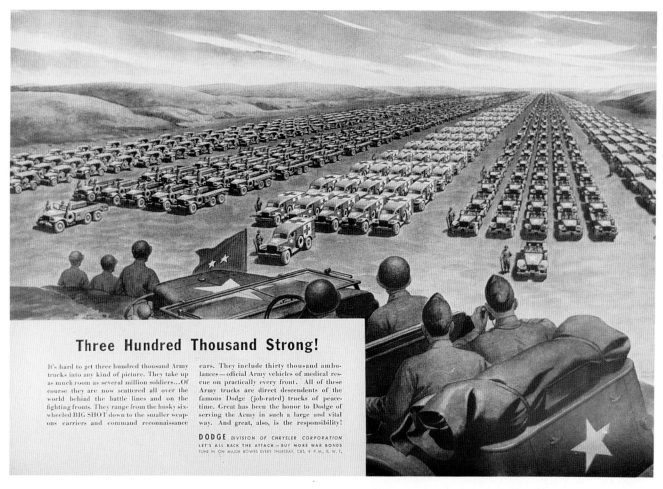

The "endless line" was a popular visual technique in posters and ads alike during the war, symbolizing limitless power and resource. In the case of this May 1944 ad, it wasn't mere hyperbole: American production had racked up some mind-boggling totals. Courtesy, Chrysler Corp.

Emergency Management, created in May 1940.) The OPM absorbed the functions of the NDAC and served as the government's coordinator of all industrial production until it was, in turn, consumed by the War Production Board (WPB).

In *Arsenal of Democracy*, Donald Nelson wrote that Knudsen "would call up the heads of some giant industry and tell them what had to be done." For example, Knudsen telephoned K. T. Keller, president of the Chrysler Company, "and told him that Chrysler had to manufacture more tanks than any corporation had ever manufactured in the past." Later, Nelson wrote, "The tanks which rolled out of the Chrysler plant were to hit the Axis all over the map, in Africa, in Russia, and in France."

The complexity of these tasks was not apparent when the massive effort was first getting geared up. Many people assumed the tank would be simple for auto makers to produce. The less technically minded planners thought that all they had to do was mount guns and armor on a tractor. Engineers and designers

quickly realized that all of that weight would crush the frames of commercial vehicles and that tanks also needed special engines and transmissions, treads, radio apparatus, guns, flamethrowers, and other special gear. At a time when the average civilian car cost about $1,000, tanks cost $45,000.

While helping produce the M-4 tank, a Ford engineer adapted an engine that had been designed for aircraft. In December 1940 the company agreed to build 400 tanks a month.

This pre-war planning did have tangible results. By 1941, General Motors was producing B-25 assemblies for North American Aviation, and Ford was mak-

Next page
This installment in Oldsmobile's insignia series appeared in February 1944, and illustrates that aviation squadrons didn't have a monopoly on gutsy designs. Courtesy, Oldsmobile Division, GMC

ing B-24 assemblies for Consolidated Aircraft Corporation. Chrysler and the Goodyear Tire & Rubber Company provided assemblies for the B-26 to the Glenn L. Martin Company. The Hudson Motor Car Company also produced fuselage assemblies for the Martin B-26.

These facts paint a deceptively smooth scenario, however. The conversion of the automobile industry was much more complicated. According to historian Lee Kennett, author of *For the Duration,* there was considerable controversy over the conversion of the auto industry, particularly during 1940. The "Reuther Plan," named after the head of the United Mine Workers, proposed that the industry make both cars and weapons. Knudsen and other federal and labor officials "openly disagreed on how rapidly and how extensively the automobile industry should be converted to armaments production," Kennett wrote. Even after Pearl Harbor, in December 1941, it was

"NOTHING'LL STOP THE ARMY AIR CORPS!"

OLDSMOBILE DIVISION OF GENERAL MOTORS

This December 1942 ad from Oldsmobile could have doubled as an AAF recruiting pitch. Note the slogan in the starburst at the bottom—World War II was a great time for slogans—as well as the ubiquitous pitch for war bonds. The P-39 featured an engine behind the cockpit and a "car door" entry system. It didn't deserve the accolades doled out in this ad's copy; the Japanese Zeros that flew against it were clearly superior. The P-39 found its niche with the Russians but stayed active in the AAF until early 1943. By 1944, it had lost its role to the P-47 and P-51 in all theaters. Courtesy, Oldsmobile Division, GMC

apparent that production in auto plants was being cut because of a shortage of materials, but the plants were not being converted to war production. "These revelations got extensive press coverage," Kennett pointed out, and Congress began a couple of investigations to determine whether there were conscious delays and, if so, why.

"Within OPM, many felt that the auto makers were purposefully dragging their feet; one of them was a man in the Information Division named Bruce Catton [later winner of a Pulitzer Prize]," Kennett said. In a memo to his division chief, Catton said, in part, "The vital question of using this industry's facilities to help save the country's life has been bitched, botched and buggered from start to finish." He felt that the heads of the auto industry were preoccupied with business as usual to an extent that was almost criminal.

Catton, of course, didn't have to deal with labor unions and American consumers. Although the auto makers were making provisional and tentative steps, delays were understandable. In late 1941, according to *Freedom's Arsenal,* "Time had not yet healed the scars left by the phrases, 'war-monger' and 'merchant of death,' which had been hurled at those industrialists who had helped arm the nation in World War I. Such phrases, derived from the Nye munitions investigations, were symptomatic of the anti-business psychology that had gripped the nation" in the 1930s.

At any rate, auto makers weren't yet of one voice. Some were cautious, others were eager, others were both at various times. Particularly unpredictable was Henry Ford, who was an ardent non-interventionist, but (as Geoffrey Perrett wrote in *Days of Sadness, Years of Triumph*) "had responded to Roosevelt's call for 50,000 planes a year by saying that he could himself turn out 1,000 planes a week; later he raised his sights to 1,000 per day." Lindbergh later called this boast "a preposterous idea." In the middle of June 1940, Ford agreed to manufacture 6,000 Rolls-Royce aircraft motors, which the American government wanted to give to the British. He then reversed himself and canceled the contract. He later refused a tentative proposal from Douglas Aircraft in August to make 2,500 bombers, but tentatively agreed in August 1940 to make 4,000 Pratt & Whitney 18-cylinder aircraft engines.

After the doldrums of the Depression, Detroit was starting to roll. Retail sales in 1941 shot up 16 percent, and automobile sales soared 40 percent. Auto makers raised their estimate of the number of cars they could make and sell, from 4,000,000 to 5,000,000 units in 1941. From business' point of view, why divert, water down, or otherwise disable the system?

As a result, "Even after Pearl Harbor the automobile companies continued to resist conversion," Perrett said, forcing the government to concede materials for another 250,000 cars. Oldsmobile's production for the 1942 models began on August 29, 1941; the company would build 67,999 1942 models.

After Pearl Harbor, events accelerated. On December 30, 1941, the AMA board of directors created the

Already building Pratt & Whitney engines and tanks, in mid-1943 Buick accepted contracts to make 500,000 75–mm shell cases. In total, Buick tackled more than 30 war-production tasks. The company made 424,000 steel cartridge

cases, nearly 20,000 tank power trains, 9.7 million 20–mm shell bodies, more than 2,500 tank destroyers, and 2,952 mounts for anti-aircraft guns. This double-page ad appeared in October 1942. Courtesy, Buick Motor Division, GMC

Automotive Council for War Production. The government banned the sale of new cars to the public on January 1, 1942. The warm-up laps, the waffling, and the jostling for position were over. It was time to start the sprint.

In the five weeks after the Japanese attack, the War Department contracted with the auto industry for $3.5 billion in military supplies, a sum that equaled the total for the two years after the Nazi invasion of Poland. That contract amount rapidly grew to $14 billion.

In short order, auto makers were contracting to make guns and shells that had never been produced in the United States. They made several types of Browning and Browning-Colt machine guns, Oerlikon and Bofors anti-aircraft cannons, Hispano-Suiza automatic aircraft cannons, tank and field artillery pieces, and carbines. They produced ordnance ranging from .30–caliber cartridge cases up to 155–mm shells, bombs, and torpedoes.

By early 1941, Ford had accepted war contracts for $480 million; an interesting minor project was the

production of fifteen- and thirty-man gliders, which it began in March 1942. The craft had a tubular steel fuselage covered by fabric and plywood wings, weighed 6,800 pounds with a full load, and could carry fifteen or thirty soldiers or a 75–mm howitzer. Ford made 4,291 of these gliders.

In September 1941, 914 of 6,407 Oldsmobile employees were working on war-related projects. By May 1942, the ratio was reversed, and only 744 out of 7,385 were at work on projects that *weren't* for the military. Late that year, the Chrysler Tank Arsenal had been built in a cornfield and was ready to turn out about 100 tanks a week. Chrysler would eventually make 59,000 Bofors anti-aircraft guns, 3.5 billion rounds of ammunition, more than 2,000 range finders, 20,000 tanks and tank destroyers, and nearly 27,000 repeater compasses.

One of Chrysler's projects shows the surprising complexity of many of the wartime jobs. The company had to design and install more than 5,000 special tools, jigs, dies, and fixtures to make the Sperry gyro-compass, a crucial device to combat the Nazi deploy-

In this May 1944 ad, the Champion Spark Plug Company used the familiar AAF insignia as an attention-getter. After the war, Champion quickly branched out into producing jet igniter cores, producing those used in the Saturn C-1 rocket, the Concorde, and F-15s and F-16s. Courtesy, Champion Spark Plug Co.

Chrysler packed plenty of information about its war production into this combat-scene ad. The fine print at the bottom mentions engines, pontoons, cannon and tank parts, aircraft wing panels, and air-raid sirens, as well as the searchlights shown in the battle scene. Courtesy, Chrysler Corp.

ment of magnetic mines in 1941. The British answer to the mines was the De Gaussing belt, which reversed a ship's magnetic field—and also destroyed the already-marginal accuracy of magnetic compasses.

Much later, when the 5,500th Sperry gyro-compass made by Chrysler's Dodge Division was delivered in February 1945, Rear Adm. E. L. Cochrane, chief of the navy's Bureau of Ships, wrote that "it will mark the completion of one of industry's war contracts originally considered impossible." Chrysler built them for 55 percent of the original estimated cost: $23.5 million instead of $42.7 million. None of the compasses were returned as defective; one faulty compass was found during tests at the factory, and it took days for inspectors to find the

Next page
The Allison Division of General Motors was another of the GM divisions that racked up significant contributions to the war effort. At its plant in Indianapolis, Allison was turning out 300 liquid-cooled engines per month by the end of 1941. Courtesy, General Motors Corp.

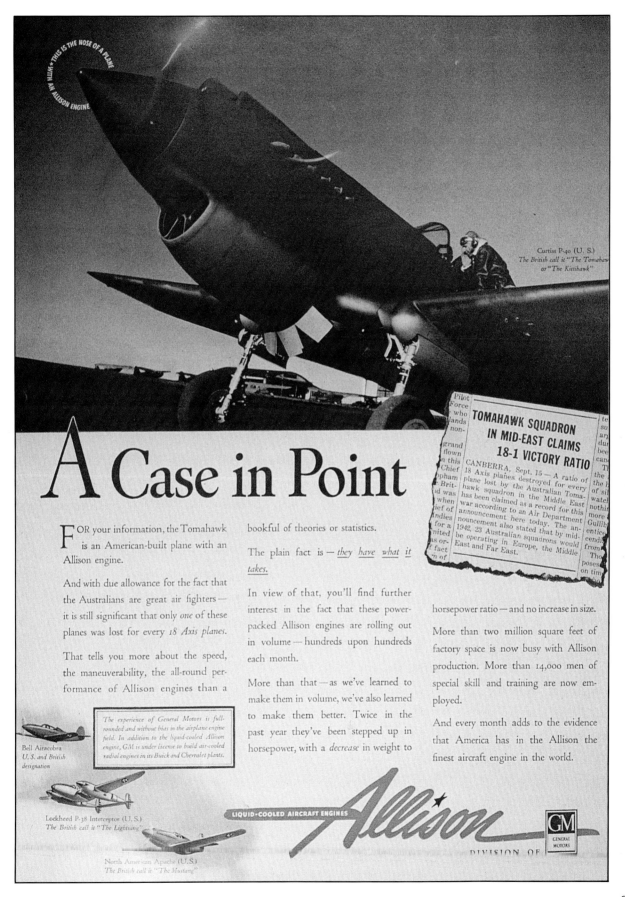

THIS IS THE NOSE OF A PLANE WITH AN ALLISON ENGINE

Curtiss P-40 (U. S.)
The British call it "The Tomahawk"
or "The Kittihawk"

A Case in Point

FOR your information, the Tomahawk is an American-built plane with an Allison engine.

And with due allowance for the fact that the Australians are great air fighters — it is still significant that only *one* of these planes was lost for every *18 Axis planes.*

That tells you more about the speed, the maneuverability, the all-round performance of Allison engines than a bookful of theories or statistics.

The plain fact is — *they have what it takes.*

In view of that, you'll find further interest in the fact that these power-packed Allison engines are rolling out in volume — hundreds upon hundreds each month.

More than that — as we've learned to make them in volume, we've also learned to make them better. Twice in the past year they've been stepped up in horsepower, with a *decrease* in weight to horsepower ratio — and no increase in size.

More than two million square feet of factory space is now busy with Allison production. More than 14,000 men of special skill and training are now employed.

And every month adds to the evidence that America has in the Allison the finest aircraft engine in the world.

The experience of General Motors is full-rounded and without bias in the airplane engine field. In addition to the liquid-cooled Allison engine, GM is under license to build air-cooled radial engines in its Buick and Chevrolet plants.

Bell Airacobra
U. S. and British
designation

Lockheed P-38 Interceptor (U. S.)
The British call it "The Lightning"

North American Apache (U.S.)
The British call it "The Mustang"

LIQUID-COOLED AIRCRAFT ENGINES *Allison*

GM GENERAL MOTORS

DIVISION OF

fault, a fleck of paint on one bearing. The bearing had been trued to one ten thousandth of an inch, and the paint was enough to disable the entire assembly. Cochrane wrote that the compasses "have seen service in every theater of operation on large landing craft and auxiliary ships so vital to the successful operation of any fleet."

Testing of the compasses was rigorous, and unusual for employees who were used to working with automobiles. The final test used Scorsby machines, "which counterfeit the roll, pitch and yaw of a ship laboring in heavy weather, counterfeit it so successfully that inspectors surrounded by a bobbing ballet of these machines were known to grow sea-sick from following the gyrations with their eyes," wrote Wesley Stout in *A War Job "Thought Impossible."*

In early 1942, Buick began designing the T-70 tank, conceived as an eight-ton, highly mobile tank destroyer. The army decided it wanted a sixteen-ton tank that would go faster and carry a larger cannon. A prototype was done in October. The army eventually ordered 1,000 of this tank, at a cost of $50 million, designating it the M-18.

Lt. Gen. Brehon Somervell, commanding general of the army's Services of Supply, toured auto factories early in 1942. He said, "The road ahead is dim with the dust of battles still unfought. How long that road is, no one can know. But it is shorter than it would have been had not our enemies misjudged us and themselves. For, when Hitler put his war on wheels he ran it straight down our alley. When he hitched his chariot to an internal combustion engine, he opened up a new battle front—a front that we know well. It's called Detroit."

At the Buick plant at Flint, Michigan, every building was soon devoted to war production. Workers there had to rework or redesign 65 percent of the automobile machine tools. From January to June 1942, the automobile industry doubled its war output; in July, 981 auto plants in thirty-one states were active in the war program.

There were setbacks, of course, particularly in view of the sweeping urgency of the times. Willow Run, near Ypsilanti, Michigan, was the Ford project that grabbed the most dismal headlines. Construction had started in March 1941. Henry Ford's grandson, Henry Ford II, came out of the navy and went back to civilian work as manager of the plant. But shortages of tools, workers, and raw materials gave it a sluggish start, made even worse by the sheer complexity of the task; cars were complicated, but the B-24 had 700,000 rivets and 1,550,000 other parts.

The original schedule had called for 100 bombers a month, which was raised in September to 205 and later to 400. As a consequence, the cost of operating the factory rose from $11 million to $47.6 million. The L-shaped building was 3,200 feet long and 1,279 feet wide, a total of about 3.5 million square feet.

In June 1942, Donald Nelson visited Willow Run, which Lee Kennett called "that limping giant." Kennett wrote, "Deadlines had been revised again: the plant would not produce its first B-24 in knockdown form until July 12; the first flyaway would not take place until September."

In January 1943, the plant produced 31 bombers; in February, 75; in March, 104—still short of the AAF's goal of 405, but at least proof that the corner had been turned. The output climbed to 254 in September, 308 in October, and 365 by the end of 1943. When Willow Run

By March 1943, more and more ads could begin getting away from the "wild blue yonder" and showing scenes of ground combat. The "somewhere in . . ." location was a popular, security-conscious description. Courtesy, General Motors Corp.

Next page
The mini-lesson in combat tactics and procedures was a standby of wartime ads. Here, Pontiac sketches how to use a 40-mm cannon. The war-bond Minute Man, in the inset at lower right, was used by the Treasury Department as a symbol throughout the war. Courtesy, Pontiac Division, GMC

Page 88
In an effort to build and maintain the morale of workers on the homefront, government posters and commercial ads all emphasized the importance of military production, often comparing workers with soldiers. Pontiac juxtaposes the stateside worker with the weapons platform at sea, a common device in wartime ads. Courtesy, Pontiac Division, GMC

PONTIAC
BUILDING FAST AND BUILDING WELL... *FOR LIBERTY*

IN 25 SECONDS, she'll be in action—throwing shells into the air at the rate of 120 a minute!

That's just one of the many, many reasons why 40 mm automatic cannon are so frequently seen in areas exposed to dive bomber attacks. Instead of being restricted to fixed positions, these remarkably versatile anti-aircraft weapons can be quickly shifted from place to place—

—whole batteries, including personnel and am-

munition, leap-frogging for miles and being emplaced and shooting again in less than an hour! And when the skies are clear but there's trouble below, the weapon becomes an automatic field gun—deadly against tanks, exposed personnel, machine guns and mortar positions. Right now, we're busy at work on *SIX* very important and widely differing war assignments. But building the 40 mm in volume is one of our *very favorite* jobs—because it's good to realize that you're giving lots of good men lots of good weapons they like!

PONTIAC DIVISION OF GENERAL MOTORS
Every Sunday Afternoon . . . GENERAL MOTORS SYMPHONY OF THE AIR—NBC Network

PONTIAC'S SIX WAR ASSIGNMENTS INCLUDE: OERLIKON 20 MM ANTI-AIRCRAFT CANNON, AIRCRAFT TORPEDOES, 40 MM FIELD GUNS, DIESEL ENGINE PARTS, TANK AXLES, TRUCK ENGINE PARTS

PONTIAC

OFFICIAL U. S. NAVY PHOTO

"RIGHT HERE IS WHERE VICTORY STARTS!"

RIGHT HERE IS WHERE VICTORY STARTS!

When we at Pontiac Motor Division undertook production of Aircraft Torpedoes, we knew and fully appreciated the manufacturing trials and problems involved. And, we were able to subscribe fully to the words of a high ranking Navy officer who described the Aircraft Torpedo as "the deadliest weapon of the sea, and *the most difficult to make...*" But we fully understood, too, the terrible urgency

with which this weapon was needed by our Navy! That is why Pontiac craftsmen hurled themselves into the job. That is why they responded so willingly to factory bulletin board messages such as the one reproduced above. And that is why, in due time, sleek, slippery and deadly Aircraft Torpedoes began emerging...began rolling from our production line.

Yes, Pontiac workmen know that "Right Here Is Where Victory Starts!"—right here where the

weapons of war are being built. But they know *it is only a start!* Our task is simply to build fast and build well, so that courageous men on the firing fronts will have the necessary tools *in volume* and *on time* to *finish the job.* To them goes full credit for the final and glorious Victory ahead!

Every Sunday Afternoon . . . GENERAL MOTORS SYMPHONY OF THE AIR—NBC Network

PONTIAC DIVISION OF GENERAL MOTORS

BUY WAR BONDS
AND STAMPS
Keep America Free!

Oerlikon 20-mm. Anti-Aircraft Cannon | Aircraft Torpedoes for the Navy | 40-mm. Automatic Field Guns | Diesel Engine Parts | Axles for M-5 Tanks | Engine Parts for Army Trucks

finally hit its stride, it was something to behold. "Parking lots were filled with workers' cars, women in coveralls mingled with Army inspectors, helmeted flyers hung about the hangars; engineers made their way to their quarters on the mezzanine floor, and union stewards and security police argued about factory conditions," wrote Allan Nevins and Frank Hill in their book *Ford*. "Already half-finished planes moved from station to station, gathering engines, guns and wings like gigantic champions donning their armor for the battle."

Willow Run would become the world's largest industrial plant, with $4 billion worth of war contracts. At its peak in 1944, it turned out a bomber every sixty-three minutes; Ford was making 48.5 percent of all the B-24s produced. When it closed in 1945, it had made 8,685 bombers, an average of 202 a month.

The famous Ford name also figured in some of the trivia of the war. Rumors (both positive and negative) were tremendously popular during wartime. In his book *Wartime*, Paul Fussell wrote that "in the Japanese prison camp at Davao, in the Philippines . . . there were two recurrent rumors collected by a man who wrote down all the rumors he heard and finally amassed a collection of some 2,000." The first was that a popular film star was dead. The second was that "Henry Ford was going to give each prisoner of war a free car when the war was over."

It was a nice fantasy, but the car makers had their hands full and didn't have time to dream up publicity ideas. Conversion was swift and output skyrocketed. In September, the auto industry was producing war material at the rate of $5.4 billion, 32 percent ahead of what had been the rate of non-military production in 1941, the peak peacetime year. The industry was hiring 40,000 new workers per month, in part to take the place of former employees now wearing military uniforms. During the war, 2,255 Oldsmobile employees joined the military, and 52 died in the line of duty; every company had a similar tale to tell.

At Saginaw, the original plan had been to have the first Browning gun finished by December 1941 and to produce forty guns by the next month, doubling that for several months. The Saginaw workers finished the first machine gun seven months early. By March 1942, when 280 weapons had been called for, they'd made 28,728, and had cut the cost of the weapon by 75 percent.

Many companies closely related to the auto industry also played significant roles. For example, the Champion Spark Plug Company had been intimately involved in the history of aviation, so it was only natural that this company would find its hands full during the war. Champion spark plugs had been used in the adapted automobile engines that powered aircraft during the early 1900s, and in the 1920s, the company developed spark plugs specifically for the aviation industry.

By 1941, Champion was making approximately one-half million spark plugs per year. During the war, it specialized in making spark plugs for fighter planes and tanks. In 1943, the company turned out 24 million plugs. In all, between 1941 and 1945, Champion produced 78 million ceramic plugs for aircraft.

For those of us who are used to specialization on the part of car and airplane manufacturers, the range of the auto industry's involvement in aviation production during the war is astonishing. Shortly after the United States entered World War II, auto plants were making parts and assemblies for American fighter aircraft: engines, propellers, automatic cannons and machine guns, instruments, and fuselage sub-assemblies. The Buick plant in Chicago produced Pratt & Whitney radial engines. Chevrolet built 10 percent of all the aircraft engines produced in the United States in 1943. The company also built landing craft, 90-mm guns, high-explosive and armor-piercing shells, and military trucks.

The DeSoto Division of Chrysler Corporation produced airplane wing sections, bomber fuselage noses and center sections, and assemblies for anti-aircraft guns and Sherman tanks. In June 1942, Ford accepted a contract to make 5,000 amphibious jeeps. In October, the auto industry had 850,000 employees, about 100,000 more than it had had during peacetime. The industry was about 85 percent converted to war work.

By December 1942, Ford was delivering 805 aircraft engines a month, compared to 700 by Nash and 600 by Pratt & Whitney itself. That month, 960,000 factory workers were punching time clocks at 775 auto plants. By May 1943, that total had risen to 1.2 million employees, of whom about 26 percent were women. Counting subcontractors and suppliers, more than 22,000 companies in 1,265 cities and 43 states were participating in the war effort as part of the automobile industry.

Pontiac was producing the Oerlikon cannon, aircraft torpedoes, tank axles, diesel marine engine parts, truck engine parts, and the Bofors 40-mm automatic field gun. The Bofors gun was the largest automatic weapon built by the Allies up to that time, capable of firing two rounds a second and of being set up in twenty-five seconds. It proved effective against tanks and dive-bombers, particularly in the North African and Italian campaigns. Torpedoes were a deceptively difficult task: they had more than 5,000 parts and were,

Next page
The text of this September 1942 ad reveals the unusual and extensive cooperation typical of the war-production effort: a car company building an aircraft engine designed by one aircraft company for an aircraft built by another.

Page 91
Texaco's World War II ads featured stark, bold images of the type more often seen on posters than in ads. Reprinted with permission of Texaco, Inc.

The proudest assignment in our 90-year history

Studebaker BUILDS WRIGHT CYCLONE ENGINES FOR THE *Flying Fortress*

At flying fields throughout the world, airmen speak with unqualified admiration of the Flying Fortress, designed by Boeing and powered with mighty Cyclone engines. Studebaker, America's oldest manufacturer of highway transportation, welcomes the opportunity to work for victory with Wright, America's oldest builder of airplane engines. The same skill, the same Studebaker plus, that have gone into every Studebaker passenger car and truck, are today going into every implement of war being produced by Studebaker. We're proud of our assignments in the arming of our United States.

★ STUDEBAKER'S 90TH ANNIVERSARY 1852-1942 ★

HEIL...!

They salute you, Fuehrer... your dead warriors.

They died... for what? Not Victory, for today the legions of decency are growing ever stronger.

Here in America, millions of peace-loving citizens are willingly skimping on food... going without gasoline... working and investing their savings to defeat you.

Our vast industrial plants are pouring out munitions in ever greater quantity.

From The Texas Company's refineries alone are coming millions of gallons of powerful 100-octane aviation gasoline... toluene for making "block-busting" bombs and shells... vast quantities of other war fuels and lubricants.

Our armies have just begun to show their real strength. Our civilians are setting new records of production. To put an end to your militarism and murder. To restore the right to *live* in peace and freedom.

THE TEXAS COMPANY
TEXACO FIRE-CHIEF & SKY-CHIEF GASOLINES · HAVOLINE & TEXACO MOTOR OILS

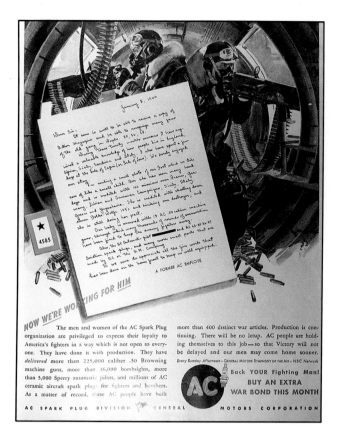

As workers left homefront factories and joined the military, they sometimes encountered products that they'd worked on back home, as this letter from a former worker at the AC Spark Plug Division of General Motors attested. The ad appeared in October 1944. Courtesy, AC Rochester Division, GMC

Like many other companies, Oldsmobile got a headstart on war production. By November 1940, it had accepted contracts to make 75-mm and 105-mm shells and had started to build a plant for that purpose. It also made landing gear parts for bombers, 220,000 articulating rods for Pratt & Whitney radial engines, and more than 27 million 105-mm shells at two of its plants. Oldsmobile made a total of 48.7 million shells of all kinds, ranging from 75-mm and three-inch shells up to 105 mm and 155 mm. From 1941 to 1946, the company tallied more than $410 million in defense sales. The company also operated the Army-Navy Gun Service School, training 10,000 service members to repair guns in the field. Courtesy, General Motors Corp.

in the words of the chief of the Naval Bureau of Ordnance, "the deadliest weapon of the sea—most difficult to make, maintain and adjust." The tank axles were the powertrain of the army's M-5 tank made by Cadillac Motor Division. Pontiac also ran an anti-aircraft training school for servicemen.

In 1943, $8.84 billion worth of war material was produced, about twice as much as the auto industry's civilian production had been in 1941. Buick alone did $391 million in war production and government work. In February of that year, Albert Speer took control of German production as minister of munitions and armaments. "Speer's effort to imitate a successful American formula was not merely too late; it was once more predicated on the fantastically erroneous notion that effective teamwork can be attained by compulsion," *Freedom's Arsenal* said.

In addition to the projects already mentioned, by 1943 the aviation work being done by auto companies reads like a who's who of flying. Auto companies were making the B-24 Liberator, Grumman TBF Avenger and F4F Wildcat, and Waco CG4 Glider. They were producing engines and assemblies for the Republic P-47 Thunderbolt and Vought F4U Corsair; assem-

blies for the Boeing B-17 Flying Fortress, Curtiss SB2C Helldiver and C-46 Commando, Consolidated C-87 Express, Douglas C-54 Skymaster, and Vought OS2U Kingfisher; engines for the North American P-51 Mustang, Bell P-39 Airacobra, Curtiss P-40 Boston, Lockheed P-38 Lightning, Vultee BT-15 Valiant, and the British Avro Lancaster, De Havilland Mosquito, and Supermarine Spitfire.

International Harvester ran an ad in June 1943 for trucks, and listed the following "major war products" it

Next page
Seventeen months later, Studebaker discussed improvements to the B-17, which it had been building for two years. The inset item about trucks demonstrates the truly global nature of the war in February 1944.

Studebaker craftsmen build engines for this latest model Flying Fortress

Here's the mightiest Boeing Flying Fortress of them all—the brand-new B-17G. At first glance, it doesn't look much different from previous Fortress models—until you notice that new turret under the bombardier's platform armed with its two devastating 50-caliber machine guns. Studebaker has the responsibility of building Wright Cyclone engines for this invincible Boeing bomber. And the assignment is a logical recognition of Studebaker's great engine-building reputation, so brilliantly exemplified for many years in the fine power plants of the famous Studebaker Champion, Commander and President cars. Studebaker engineers, production experts and craftsmen fully recognize the urgent needs of our armed forces for more and more of the war equipment required for decisive victory. That's why they're sparing no effort on any of their wartime assignments—the Wright Cyclone engines for the Flying Fortress, the big multiple-drive military trucks and the other vital matériel they've been delegated to produce.

Studebaker builds tens of thousands of big, multiple-drive military trucks—They've been in the thick of the fighting on the Russian front. They're serving the United Nations from Alaska to the Middle East and from the British Isles to India. Studebaker is now one of the world's largest manufacturers of big military trucks.

★ BUY U. S. WAR BONDS ★

Awarded to Aviation Division  *of The Studebaker Corporation*

Studebaker BUILDS CYCLONE ENGINES FOR THE BOEING FLYING FORTRESS

93

© 1944, The Studebaker Corporation

"Those engines sure have the power!"

THE brother of a waist gunner on a Boeing Flying Fortress wrote Studebaker quoting him as saying:

"Those Wright Cyclone engines that Studebaker builds are really dependable and sure have the power."

Comments like that are fully appreciated, of course. But Studebaker men and women know that what count most are the accomplishments of the stout-hearted air crews and rugged ground crews of our country's warplanes and the achievements of our fighting forces everywhere.

In fact, whatever amount of satisfaction the Studebaker organization may derive from the extent and consequence of its war work is always tempered by the realization that Studebaker is only one unit in a vast American fighting and producing team where everyone's effort is important.

Studebaker takes pride in its assignments on that team. Huge quantities of Wright Cyclone engines for the Boeing Flying Fortress—big multiple-drive military trucks—and other units of vital war matériel continue to stream forth from the five great Studebaker factories.

Unsung Hero OF OUR NAVY

Aerial radio gunner in a Navy dive bomber! One of the toughest jobs of all! Let's show him we're for him and

BUY MORE BONDS

Studebaker BUILDS WRIGHT CYCLONE ENGINES FOR THE BOEING FLYING FORTRESS

had built: half-track military vehicles, torpedoes,
artillery prime movers, automatic airplane cannons,
Oerlikon gun mounts, aerodrome control trucks,
armored scout car hulls, high-speed 155-mm gun carriages, gun loaders, airplane engine-cowling assemblies, tank transmissions, blood-bank refrigerators,
shells, gun carriages, adapter boosters, trackers, and
Marine Corps invasion ice chests. "When the story of
this war is written, trucks will contribute one of the
most glorious chapters," the ad boasted.

February 1944 saw the second anniversary of the
cessation of civilian production. The auto industry had
made $14.2 billion worth of war materials and was
humming along at an annual production rate of $10.5
billion. Auto makers had produced, so far, $5 billion
worth of aircraft and aircraft parts, $4.2 billion worth
of military vehicles and parts, and $1.9 billion worth of
tanks.

By October 1944, the AC Spark Plug Division of
General Motors had delivered more than 225,000 .50-
caliber Browning machine guns, 16,000 bombsights,
5,000 Sperry automatic pilots, and millions of ceramic
spark plugs for fighters and bombers.

As amazing as those totals are, even they don't
reveal the extent of the full contribution. A June 1945
survey found that 374,000 men and women from the
auto industry had entered the service. "Nearly every

*In this photo from a book published just after the war and
now long out of print, employees of the AC Spark Plug
Division of General Motors make .50-caliber machine guns at
their factory, which once produced spark plugs only. The
photo's original caption said, "The first plant outside of the
small arms industry in the East to produce .50 calibre Browning machine guns, AC has been mass-producing them since
before Pearl Harbor. Now, for the first time in firearms'
history, machine guns 'come off the line' like motor cars—or
spark plugs." Courtesy, AC Rochester Division, GMC*

*In May 1944, Pontiac offered what must be the most attractive
selection of service people ever assembled. The handsome
soldier at upper right appeared by himself on another Pontiac
ad. Although this ad centers on military people, that wasn't
always the case with Pontiac ads. "Many of Pontiac's wartime
ads were directed at the women of America offering helpful
hints on taking care of 'his' car for the duration," noted Donald
Nelson in* Freedom's Arsenal. *Courtesy, Pontiac Division,
GMC*

"HELL-RAZOR"

HELL RAZORS

automotive war worker—from the desks of management to the shop benches—had a close relative under
arms," *Freedom's Arsenal* reported. "At one plant,
three employees—a tool maker, an assembler of aircraft engines, and a parts-distribution supervisor—
each reported five sons in uniform." The 301st Ordnance Regiment was composed largely of former
General Motors dealers, salesmen, and mechanics.

By the war's end, auto makers had produced 39
percent of all aircraft, subassemblies, and parts; 30
percent of all military vehicles and parts; one-third of
all machine guns; 80 percent of all tanks and tank parts;
and one-half of all diesel engines that were turned out
by American industry as a whole.

On VE Day, May 8, 1945, the WPB finally relaxed
the production controls over the auto industry, and on
May 24, authorized production of 200,000 autos in 1945.
Gasoline allotments were increased. It was time to get
back to business as usual.

Another AAF squadron grabs the spotlight in May 1944, using
cannons made by the company that produced this ad. Courtesy, General Motors Corp.

Next page
At their best, wartime ads were uniquely informative, particularly in comparison to today's nebulous, image-is-everything
productions. In this striking series, Oldsmobile taught colorful lessons in tactics, recognized an actual squadron, tipped its
hat to its own contributions, and made a pitch for war bonds.
It also illustrated and explained squadron insignia, one of the
uniquely colorful aspects of military aviation both during the
war and today. This ad appeared in November 1943. Courtesy, General Motors Corp.

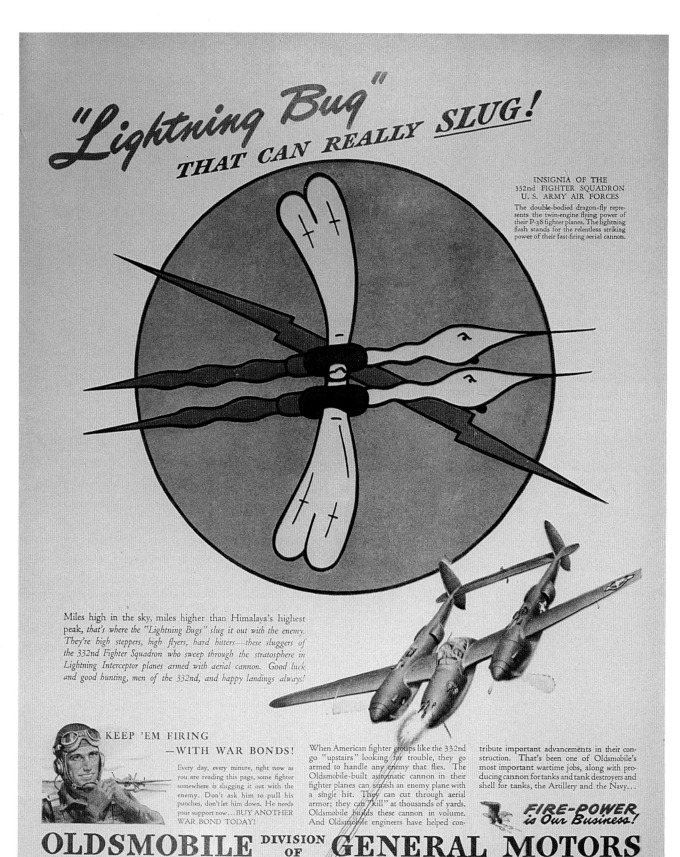

"Lightning Bug" THAT CAN REALLY SLUG!

INSIGNIA OF THE
332nd FIGHTER SQUADRON
U. S. ARMY AIR FORCES

The double-bodied dragon-fly represents the twin-engine flying power of their P-38 fighter planes. The lightning flash stands for the relentless striking power of their fast-firing aerial cannon.

Miles high in the sky, miles higher than Himalaya's highest peak, that's where the "Lightning Bugs" slug it out with the enemy. They're high steppers, high flyers, hard hitters—these sluggers of the 332nd Fighter Squadron who sweep through the stratosphere in Lightning Interceptor planes armed with aerial cannon. Good luck and good hunting, men of the 332nd, and happy landings always!

KEEP 'EM FIRING
—WITH WAR BONDS!

Every day, every minute, right now as you are reading this page, some fighter somewhere is slugging it out with the enemy. Don't ask him to pull his punches, don't let him down. He needs your support now...BUY ANOTHER WAR BOND TODAY!

When American fighter groups like the 332nd go "upstairs" looking for trouble, they go armed to handle any enemy that flies. The Oldsmobile-built automatic cannon in their fighter planes can smash an enemy plane with a single hit. They can cut through aerial armor; they can "kill" at thousands of yards. Oldsmobile builds these cannon in volume. And Oldsmobile engineers have helped con-

tribute important advancements in their construction. That's been one of Oldsmobile's most important wartime jobs, along with producing cannon for tanks and tank destroyers and shell for tanks, the Artillery and the Navy...

FIRE-POWER is Our Business!

OLDSMOBILE DIVISION OF GENERAL MOTORS

KEEP 'EM FIRING

98

© 1945 The Studebaker Corporation

It's a jungle "Weasel" too!

IN the forbidding tropical undergrowth of the Pacific islands, Studebaker's amazing new Weasel personnel and cargo carrier is now in action with our armed forces.

It's advancing, as it has been doing in Europe, over terrain that seems impossible for any mechanized military vehicle to negotiate.

Swiftly and stealthily, the Weasel glides forward in mud and swamp as well as on sand and snow. And it floats like a boat in lakes and rivers, as its powerful Studebaker Champion engine propels it from shore to shore.

A many-purpose vehicle, this new "Champion" in invasion warfare not only transports men and supplies but also serves to carry wounded back to hospital areas. It's geared to clamber up seemingly impossible grades on its flexible rubber-padded tracks. With its help, light artillery pieces,

and the ammunition to feed them, can often be moved up to otherwise inaccessible positions.

Built by Studebaker and powered by the famous Studebaker Champion engine, the Weasel is just one of a number of Studebaker war production assignments which include Wright Cyclone engines for the famous Boeing Flying Fortress as well as heavy-duty Studebaker military trucks.

Awarded To All  *Studebaker Plants*

Studebaker
PIONEER AND PACEMAKER IN AUTOMOTIVE PROGRESS

Now building Wright Cyclone engines for the Boeing Flying Fortress—heavy-duty Studebaker military trucks—the Army's versatile personnel and cargo carrier, the Weasel.

Your War Bonds help keep the Flying Fortresses flying

Keep on buying War Bonds and keep the War Bonds you buy. They're the world's best investment. Every $3 you invest pays you back $4.

Students of history could chart the progress of the war from ads such as this one, as the Pacific island-hopping campaign picked up steam. The ocean atoll in the inset picture is also distinctive of that theater of war. The Weasel was an ordnance cargo carrier designated M-29, which cost $4,815.

99

Studebaker's big military trucks stand out in all the major war zones

IN virtually every theater of this global war, mighty military trucks produced by Studebaker are moving the men and supplies of the United Nations.

From the Alcan highway to the Russian front, from Africa to China, tens of thousands of big, powerful Studebakers are writing brilliant new pages of transport history.

The stand-up stamina, for which these rugged Studebaker trucks are already world-famed, is nothing new. It's as old as the Studebaker business. It goes back more than 91 years to the days when the Studebaker brothers made the phrase, "give more than you promise," the watchword for all Studebaker activities.

In this war, for the sixth time in a

national emergency, Studebaker is supplying military transport on a large scale—in fact, Studebaker is now one of the world's leading builders of big, multiple-drive military trucks. Studebaker is also producing great quantities of Wright Cyclone engines for the Boeing Flying Fortress as well as much other vital war matériel.

Obviously, no new passenger cars or trucks for civilian needs are being made at Studebaker now. The all-important job is military production. But finer Studebaker trucks and passenger cars will be available to the public, once decisive victory is accomplished. And, you may be sure, they will be outstanding examples of brilliant engineering and sound manufacturing.

BUY U. S. WAR BONDS

SEND 10¢ FOR A BEAUTIFUL REPRINT OF THIS FLYING FORTRESS PAINTING

This dramatic picture of a Flying Fortress is available in 24x22 inch size on a special stock suitable for framing, free from advertising. If you wish one, address Studebaker, South Bend, Indiana, enclosing 10¢ to cover mailing cost.

This June 1943 ad offers the "Proudest Assignment" artwork as a free poster, as well as an interesting European scene.

100

On every fighting front *Fisher*

The Army-Navy "E" flies above four Fisher plants for excellence in aircraft production and from two others for tank production, while the Navy "E," with four stars, is flown by still another Fisher plant for its naval ordnance work.

THE men who do the fighting, whether on land, sea or in the air, know how important it is to have the best equipment.

They realize that the work we do in our factories can, if done well enough, give them a combat advantage.

We realize that, too. That's why we are devoting all the skills we have developed, all the crafts we have mastered, to give our armed forces the all-important edge.

Whether it's a plane, an anti-aircraft gun, a tank, or a highly sensitive flying instrument, each gets every technical plus we can give it — and that's several.

Craftsmanship is a Fisher tradition. And today we believe craftsmanship carries a particular punch of its own to give a fighting man a break when a break is more than welcome.

Every Sunday Afternoon
GENERAL MOTORS SYMPHONY OF THE AIR
NBC Network

armament
BODY BY *Fisher*

D I V I S I O N   O F   G E N E R A L   M O T O R S

Fisher Body Division of General Motors operated a tank plant at Grand Blanc, Michigan; the company also made B–25 assemblies for North American. By early 1945, Fisher Body Division had produced 16,000 tanks and tank destroyers. This ad appeared in January 1944. Courtesy, General Motors Corp.

U. S. RANGERS... Hand-picked and especially trained, they're a swift-moving, hard-hitting outfit. Here's one in his "business-suit," camouflaged and invisible at thirty feet

But there's no hiding Chesterfield's MILDER BETTER TASTE

Here's real smoking ammunition tucked in the pockets of our fighting men, ready for instant service. Where a cigarette counts most, Chesterfield serves smokers well with its *Right Combination* of the world's best cigarette tobaccos.

For Mildness .. for Better Taste and Cooler Smoking .. make your next pack ...

CHESTERFIELD

RECOGNIZED EVERYWHERE
THE CIGARETTE THAT GIVES SMOKERS
WHAT THEY WANT

Copyright 1943
LIGGETT & MYERS
TOBACCO CO.

★ ★ ★ DON'T HIDE YOUR DOLLARS ★ ENLIST THEM WITH UNCLE SAM ★ BUY U. S. WAR BONDS FOR VICTORY ★ ★ ★

102

Chapter 4

The War Advertising Council

"Straight Down Our Alley"

Although Americans had mixed opinions about jumping into the war in Europe, planning for huge increases in production (and its inescapable attendant, advertising) began very early. In 1941, federal officials were already beating the drums about the role that advertisers could play in the coming storm.

In a speech to the American Association of Advertising Agencies, a Commerce Department official said, "The current and prospective achievements of our production machinery are a challenge to men engaged in distribution, a challenge that ought to taste like raw meat and straight, strong liquor to you. . . . Is there a place for advertising in the future? Assuredly so." And one of the main ways that advertisers could participate, he continued, is in facing the necessity "that the nearness and the greatness of our danger be brought home—clearly, coldly, and precisely to every American. . . . use your experience and imagination to tell that story to the people." This speech was entitled "Advertising—Preserving the American Way of Life" when it was later reprinted.

These stirring tones were right for the times and wouldn't have troubled the key players in the Allied

Previous page
Chesterfield gave this May 1943 ad a military aura with camouflage writing. According to tobacco historian Harris Lewine in his book Good-Bye to All That, *"every available tobacco scrap was packaged and sold" during the war. Cigarettes were wildly popular. President Roosevelt, who had smoked a pipe since the 1920s, switched to cigarettes; national consumption zoomed from 189 billion in 1940 to 369 billion in 1947. From 1941 to 1945, 222.6 billion cigarettes (18 percent of production) were sent overseas. Lewine wrote, "Bill Mauldin might have sold more cigarettes than Bogart and all of Hollywood. His* Stars and Stripes *cartoons of dog-face noncoms 'Willie and Joe' always slogging forward, bitching, bristle-bearded, with a lit or unlit 'butt' protruding—were 'the way it was' for the World War II foot soldier." Courtesy, Liggett Group, Inc.*

cause: Churchill and Roosevelt. In his book *The Golden Fleece,* Joseph Seldin points out that in 1924, Winston Churchill had toasted the International Advertising Conference in London. "Advertising nourishes the consuming power of men," Churchill said. "It creates wants for a better standard of living. . . . It spurs individual exertion and greater production." In 1931, when Roosevelt was governor of New York, he told the Advertising Federation of America, "If I were starting life over again. . . . I would go into the advertising business in preference to almost any other."

Did advertisers succeed in telling the story "clearly" and "precisely," as the Commerce Department official had declared? There is no single answer, rather a range of answers, from a resounding "yes" to an equally emphatic "no." Some ads were extremely effective, some were odd, still others silly or ridiculous.

In 1942, the Department of Commerce continued its barrage of stirring appeals to advertisers. "All companies—small, medium and large—have a story to tell," one message said. "Seldom, in fact, has there been such a fund of material. Dramatic, inspiring, yet factual material. As partners in the vast war effort, businessmen can win the continued respect of their public. They can do this by telling the story of what they are doing and of what the people can do to help win the victory. Such advertising is urgently needed. Such advertising is plain common sense."

Appeals such as these paid off. The July 1941 issue of the *Ayer News Files,* the company newsletter of the N. W. Ayer & Son Advertising Company, pointed out that "the advertising for Michigan Bell Telephone Company has shifted to a 'defense comes first' theme." A report from the Florida Citrus Commission said, "On December 22, 1941, the commissioners decided that 'Buy a Bond' should appear in their advertising." In January 1942, the Wrigley Company announced that all the programs it sponsored had adopted defense-related themes. The 1942 annual report from the National Dairy Products Corporation said, "National Dairy's nation-wide radio programs—'Kraft Music Hall,' Kraft's

The Stetson Hat Company made parachutes, heavy webbing for parachute harnesses and safety belts, and hats for the WACs. Two grandsons of the company's founder gave their lives during World War II. One long-time Stetson employee, now retired, recalled that the company made fur-felt hats of the type now associated with drill instructors and Smokey the Bear. According to Paul Guilden of the Stetson Company, a postwar survey of Europe found that the two best-known American brands were Stetson hats and Jockey shorts. This March 1943 ad stresses security, a common theme in war posters. Courtesy, John B. Stetson Co.

'The Great Gildersleeve,' and the 'Sealtest Village Store'—had an important influence on sales, and often were used as vehicles for Government appeals." "All our advertising campaigns served the war effort by carrying to millions of readers and listeners appeals to purchase war bonds and information sponsored by the Government," the 1943 report added.

Trade associations became extremely conscious of the public's perception of their contributions to the war effort, reflecting results and trends in trade and public service publications. In 1942, a public-opinion survey by the Association of American Railroads (AAR) asked

A spectrum of emotional tones ranged through wartime ads: grim and hysterical, corny and heartwarming, or (rarely) whimsical and comic. Soldiers often appeared locked in deadly aerial combat or dodging artillery during amphibious assaults, but this ad shows the only instance of them drilling with dairy products. The ad appeared in July 1943. That year, one-sixth of the National Dairy Products Corporation's total sales were for war purposes, including direct sales to the military and Lend-Lease purchases. Their products included 122 million pounds of cheese and "3.5 million cans of Tashonka" that was "produced for the Russian Army." Courtesy, Kraft General Foods, Inc.

people "what sort of job the railroads were doing in the war." In 1941, 23 percent had no opinion and 56 percent thought the railroads were doing a good job. In 1942, however, only 12 percent had no opinion and 82 percent thought the railroads were doing a good job. AAR-produced booklets during 1942 included 100,000 copies of Count This Army In and The Iron Horse Delivers the Tools of War.

The general growth in advertising during the war is documented by the activity of this trade association,

Next page
The mention of older cars in this May 1945 ad was particularly apt—no new cars for civilians had been produced since February 1942. Courtesy, Mobil Corp.

104

Oil "Know-how" that Answered Combat Problems_

CAN HELP SOLVE SPRINGTIME CAR PROBLEMS FOR YOU!

Protect Your Car the Quality Way— Change to Summer **Mobiloil**

IN SWELTERING HEAT, under grueling combat strain, U.S. Army equipment stands up magnificently because our Army experts do a magnificent job of regular, scientific servicing.

What better lesson for U.S. motorists . . . whose older cars need Complete Summer Servicing right now!

Get complete Mobilubrication today!

Your Mobilgas dealer uses Mobiloil and Mobilgreases from the same refineries which have supplied millions of barrels of fine petroleum products to the Armed Forces . . . applies them scientifically, following a chart of your make of car.

Engine, radiator, gears, chassis are thoroughly protected...and with this service goes a careful gas-saving check-up of spark plugs, air cleaner and other important car parts. Older cars need better care. *Get it* at Mobilgas dealers!

SOCONY-VACUUM OIL COMPANY, INC. and Affiliates: Magnolia Petroleum Company, General Petroleum Corp. of California.

Official U.S. Navy Photo

Tune in
"INFORMATION PLEASE"
Sponsored by your Mobilgas Dealer
Monday Evenings, 9:30 E.W.T.—NBC

FOR QUALITY PROTECTION_ Mobiloil Mobilgas SOCONY-VACUUM Mobiloil **_And Complete Mobilubrication**

The oil that's poison...to the Japs

This Jap ship is about to become a memory.

Half a mile away, and sixty feet below the surface, a voice with a Yankee twang will announce: "Two bull's-eyes! Take her down, Tommy".

That's an American submarine at work. She's come 3800 miles from her base—and has 3800 more miles to go to get home. The responsibility for seventy highly-trained American sea fighters and their $8,000,000 weapon rests on her great Diesel engines.

The responsibility for those Diesels rests, to a large extent, on an amazing new detergent oil that lubricates them.

That oil has boosted the odds on their get-

ting to Japan's doorstep—and back—without engine trouble.

For it won't permit carbon to form beyond almost microscopic particles. They're prevented from "ganging up" to form the larger, gummy masses that clog lubrication holes, and ruin bearings; that cling to valves and make them stick; that cake, and cut down engine efficiency.

No, these tiny particles are held in suspension and rendered harmless. They actually are *drained out* at every oil-change, leaving the engine almost factory-clean!

Oils with detergent characteristics were developed by America's petroleum industry. Tide Water Associated, together with the other oil

companies, is now producing such oils in required quantities. There is no rivalry about it. We are concerned only with providing the Army and Navy with all they need for any purpose whatsoever — with perhaps a little over for essential civilian commercial use.

For the country's oil refiners are fighting as a unit. We have, where necessary, pooled equipment, shared patents and processes, in order to make our efforts most effective.

For ordinary business can't matter as much as the business that is taking American lads abroad. Our most important enterprise now is helping speed the day when they'll come back to us.

TIDE WATER ASSOCIATED OIL COMPANY
New York   Tulsa   San Francisco

WORLD'S LARGEST REFINERS OF PENNSYLVANIA OILS

TIDE WATER ASSOCIATED

GASOLINE POWERS THE ATTACK — DON'T WASTE A DROP

BUY WAR BONDS AND STAMPS!

Previous page
Oil was one of the myriad commodities that "went to war," along with food, wire, rubber, and the rest. This May 1944 ad presents the classic combination of combat documentary, technical information about the product, "we're doing our part" data, and a plea for conservation.

which included in its annual report data about the number of advertisements it had placed in national and business magazines. It tallied 80 insertions of 12 ads in 12 magazines in 1940, 132 insertions of 13 ads in 12 magazines in 1941, 137 insertions of 17 ads in 14 magazines, in 1942, 204 insertions of 17 ads in 23 magazines in 1943, and 285 insertions of 14 ads in 28 magazines in 1944. The number of insertions and the number of target magazines more than doubled during the war.

The government's grandest statement of the role of ads probably appeared in *Advertising and Its Role in War and Peace*, a Department of Commerce book issued in 1943 and crammed with a dense mixture of factual data and official cheerleading. According to the book's introduction, "Advertising is a vital cog in our free enterprise system, a potent medium for distributing information." It could help the government inform the public "of the part it must play to hasten the day of Victory. . . . With the attack on Pearl Harbor, the Department of Commerce immediately recognized that advertising would be a major weapon on the home front. . . . Talents used so effectively in creating a desire for goods could with equal effectiveness show how to help win the war."

In countries such as England, advertising waned during the war years. When war broke out, "the British advertising industry acted with resolution and dispatch," wrote humorist George Begley in *Keep Mum! Advertising Goes to War.* "They fired many of their staff, cut the pay of the survivors and prepared for years of misery. At the same time they looked round the countryside for premises unlikely to be bombed."

The Blitz gave British advertisers themes that wouldn't appear in Yank ads. "Sleep inducers seized an unparalleled opportunity," Begley pointed out. "At a time when hindrances to sleep such as bombs, fires, explosions, fear, anxiety, and shortages of food were rife as never before, Bournvita, Horlicks and Ovaltine promised in the largest spaces they could get to assist anyone who valued sleep to a deep, dreamless slumber with much soothing talk."

Some observers and analysts predicted a similar ad slump in America. In fact, the reverse would prove to be true. Radio prospered, partly because of the paper shortage, which meant that magazines could no longer accommodate all potential advertisers. The media divvied up national advertising this way: 34.4 percent newspaper, 32.2 percent magazine, and 25.4 percent radio. A study in May 1943 used 1939 as the index year, assigning the ad levels during that year a value of 100. Compared to that year, newspaper advertising had declined from an index of 106 in 1941 to 100 in 1942; radio ads, however, had soared to 128 in 1941 and 139 in 1942; and magazine advertising climbed to 119 in 1941, with a slight decline to 117 in 1942. Nevertheless, in that year, magazines took over first place. Total ad revenues for all media climbed to $2.9 billion by 1945, leading one historian to conclude, "As for the economy in general, war was good business for advertising." For some corporations, advertising costs became the largest single item in their business.

By May 1943, government advertising specialist Kenneth Davis wrote, "The conversion of industry from consumer to war production threatened to make advertising an early war casualty. It took an equally drastic conversion within advertising itself to avert the impending calamity."

The official government cheerleading, combined with the average American's sentiment about winning the war once the country entered it for real, created a juggernaut of war-oriented ads. According to one study, in 1942, roughly one-half to three-quarters of all ads didn't mention the war. During 1943 and 1944, however, one-half to three-quarters did mention the war. By 1944, advertisers were investing $100 million more in magazines than in 1942.

As a result, part way into the war, one federal analyst wrote, "It is practically impossible today to read through any publication or listen to any series of radio programs without coming upon examples of the new advertising technique." A census of the war-related ads in two random issues of one magazine shows that in August 1942, forty-eight ads were not related to the war, and only twenty-three ads were (although they included some full-page, colorful ones). In February 1943, thirty-seven ads weren't related to war themes, and thirty-six were.

The contrast is most dramatic if you compare the wartime approach with the contents of a pre-war magazine. For example, in 1940, as this ad for a Ford V–8 shows, no one was worried about gas mileage: "It's most fun, first-hand. See what this big car really has under its hood." The cartoon owner of the car says, "Boy, you shoulda seen me breeze by Doc Tompkins, comin' up Elm Street hill!" Car ads would disappear during the war, and people wouldn't have had the gas to burn, anyway.

An article in the February 1940 issue of *Life* is entitled, "A German bomber sinks an unarmed fishing trawler in the North Sea." The accompanying copy says the photos were "released by Germany as a frank admission of its policy of sinking any British ship that in

Next page
Juxtapositions of daily life stateside and on the combat fronts were common during the war, although rarely as elaborate as in this February 1944 ad from the Can Manufacturers' Institute. Note the tiger or shark mouth on the aircraft at upper right, and the unusual presence of a black man at lower left (in a typically subservient role).

WHAT CONTAINER
can match this score...

★★★ ON THE FIGHTING FRONT!

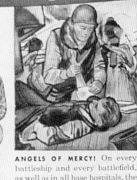

ANGELS OF MERCY! On every battleship and every battlefield, as well as in all base hospitals, the wounded get prompt care with supplies in handy form kept safe and sterile in cans—bandages . . . sulfa . . . merciful morphine . . . precious blood plasma. We are proud indeed of the part cans thus play in relieving pain, controlling infection, and saving lives in this war.

RUGGED CATERERS! America's fighting forces are the best fed in the world—and it could not happen without cans! On land and sea in the four quarters of the globe . . . in torrid heat and arctic cold . . . through jungles, over mountains, deserts, and shell-torn roads . . . food supplies flow safely to our men in the only containers which can stand up under such rough handling.

STRIKING POWER! Fuel and ammunition in the right places at the right time are essentials of war strategy. Gasoline, oil, many gun and machine parts are packed in cans because cans are sturdy, non-porous, non-inflammable and easy to handle. To such war needs we at home are sacrificing temporarily the popular can for scores of items like tooth powder, shortening, paint, and dog food.

A FIGHTING CHANCE! Canned signal flares and canned fishing tackle may sound strange. But these, with canned food and first-aid kits, are standard life-raft equipment which give men from stricken ships their chance to survive. Such items are packed in cans because cans give the only sure protection against damage from breakage, air, moisture and extremes of temperature.

★★★ ON THE HOME FRONT!

PEACETIME CONVENIENCE! No container rivals the familiar "tin" can (actually over 98% steel . . . less than 2% tin) for sturdy, lightweight, tamper-proof convenience. We took these virtues for granted when cans were plentiful —but shortage now sharpens our appreciation! So let's use wisely, without waste, whatever still comes in cans—and turn empty cans in for salvage.

FLAVOR LOCKED IN! Because cans lock out light, air, and moisture, they lock in color and flavor. That is why they are the ideal containers for such things as tobacco, coffee, spices, and cocoa, which lose their flavor as their fragrance fades. The cans formerly used for such things have a fighting job to do now, but we'll enjoy the luxury of having them back—after Victory!

FOOD VARIETY! Cans bring garden, orchard, farm and deep-sea luxuries inexpensively to our tables wherever we live, the year around . . . give first aid to nutritious meal planning. And modern canning methods capture these foods at the peak of their goodness . . . process them so expertly that they actually retain more vitamins and more minerals than do many home-cooked "fresh" foods.

PRECIOUS! In spite of the tremendous demand for cans on the war front, quantities must still be made for civilian uses — especially for foods like canned milk, important to health. Dramatically today's events are proving there is often no successful substitute for the inexpensive, hard-to-break, easy-to-ship-store-open use-and-dispose-of, thoroughly-protective can!

CAN MANUFACTURERS' INSTITUTE, INC., NEW YORK

NO OTHER CONTAINER PROTECTS LIKE THE CAN

AFTER VICTORY — THEY'LL ALL BE BACK!

108

any way helps England win the war." But even with these somber events in the spotlight, advertisements still had the time and energy for silliness. A 1940 General Electric ad shows a man talking about lightbulbs to a lifesize, female display card, which comes to life to teach him about bulbs. He ends up inviting her to a movie. This comical approach would also virtually disappear. Later in the war, this ad would show a sailor teaching his two sons how to tie knots.

In contrast to these vignettes from 1940, Pearl Harbor brought both minor and major changes to headlines, features, and domestic print ads. In November 1942, a small headline at the bottom of a Bendix ad said, "Out to War—Back Later." A Barbasol ad in March 1943 tells "What to wear to the U.S.O."

"When little Jack builds a war-stamp display booth—and gives himself a nasty dig—you know it's important to keep out germs and infection, Mother," observed one Band-Aid ad. The hero of an ad for Pabst Blue Ribbon was "Monsieur B., a musician of worldwide renown" who "gave a War Relief Concert in Blue Ribbon town. . . . The hall was sold out—how the money rolled in! The Fund Chairman's face wore a gratified grin." Some ads seemed to stretch the war's effects into every conceivable arena. One ad promised to explain "How war effects every slice of bread you buy."

Some ads became merely tinged with wartime concerns; others went right to the front lines, sometimes graphically so. A Stromberg-Carlson ad from 1942 was called "Conversation in Hell!" It read, "Imagine holding a telephone conversation . . . in a roaring bomber flying through an anti-aircraft barrage . . . in a clanging, jolting tank under fire . . . in a shell hole with screaming bombs falling on all sides!" A small inset picture shows a soldier talking on a combat radio (aircraft and explosions are visible through the window). "Hello, Central, give me no-man's-land!" he shouts.

The American Gas Association was another national trade group that advertised during the war, issuing this ad in September 1942. In an article called "A Trip Down Memory Main" in the June 1990 issue of American Gas magazine, Timothy Kelley noted that the AGA produced a series of ads that small gas companies could customize for local use. "One such ad shows Adolf Hitler painting 'Verboten' on gas cooking equipment, suggesting that Germany's leader would keep American housewives from cooking with gas if he could. You might say that logic itself is doing Army calistenics in 1942," Kelley wrote. That ad and this one both carried the AGA's 1942 slogan: "The Wonder Fuel for Cooking Now Speeds War Production." Courtesy, American Gas Assoc.

Caricaturists got more mileage out of this trio than any other targets; in time, Hitler would be no more than a moustache, and Hirohito a pair of buckteeth. The text of this ad deals with enemy propaganda, an unusual theme for ads but a common topic of war posters. The ad appeared in August 1942. Courtesy, Rockwell International Corp.

It Takes a Heap of Shootin' To Make An Ace

In Peace as in War, America Relies On Western

When quail burst from cover with a startling whir-r of wings, thoughts turn to yesterday's wonderful hunts. You recall days when the dogs were working like champions, and it seemed you *couldn't* miss.

No one knows how soon those times will come again. But when they do, you will be able to hunt quail and other upland game with Western Xpert shells in your gun. They will provide plenty of "reach" and a satisfying walloping impact.

It isn't easy to train every reflex of the eye, brain and trigger-finger to split-second coordination . . . to blast the enemy streaking in at 400 miles an hour. Cracking down on fast-flying targets wasn't new to lots of our aerial gunners. They'd spent many a great day, bird-shooting or bustin' "clay" targets. Now, clay target shooting, using shot shells, is part of every aerial gunner's training.

Western is proud to have a part in their training and fighting. Now, as in two previous wars, Western has converted its production to military ammunition. In addition to supplying millions of shot shells, more than *9 billion* cartridges have been manufactured in Western-operated plants.

Yes, it takes a heap of shootin' to make an Ace . . . and mountains of ammunition to win a war. Western Cartridge Company, East Alton, Ill.

WORLD CHAMPION AMMUNITION

SHOT SHELLS · CARTRIDGES · TRAPS AND TARGETS

110

Ads didn't convert to wartime themes without difficulty and dispute. Three years earlier, with war still on the horizon, American advertisers faced changes to their notion of "business as usual" that were in some ways more drastic than those of industry. Every factory would have a job to do, but with looming shortages of paper and ad space, not every advertiser would fit. Some people questioned whether advertising was necessary at all.

Within the advertising industry, experts argued and formulated their own priorities. James Webb Young, author of *The Diary of an Ad Man*, noted, "Every advertiser now seems to be struggling with the formulation of a policy for rationing the amount of advertising space he has left to sell.... I would give first priority to the advertisers with merchandise and services to sell; second to the advertisers, new or old, with a genuine war service message; third to the advertisers who have demonstrated a consistent purpose to maintain or build a postwar reputation. Away down at the bottom I would put those advertisers who are obviously squandering tax money on unmitigated bellywash."

The federal government, then in the business of enlisting every available resource into the war effort, accepted advertising as a handy, effective communications tool. In September 1943, the Department of Commerce documented the pervasiveness of war-oriented themes in advertising by sponsoring an exhibit of wartime advertising that drew entries from 277 companies. More than 44 percent were from what were then called "industrialists": makers of building materials, machinery, electrical goods, hardware, paints, boats, engines, tires, and gasoline. The dominant ads, in terms of size, color, number, and graphic qualities, came from both aircraft manufacturers and the automobile industry (which, in 1915, had taken the lead among national advertisers, but relinquished it around 1940 to the food industry).

The exhibit contained newspaper and magazine ads, posters, and car cards (tiny posters displayed in trolleys and buses). The organizers duly tabulated the frequency of topics in the ads:

As hundreds of thousands of Americans joined the military services, some of the country's most familiar commercial characters also enlisted in various homefront campaigns. Here, the Campbell Soup Kid presents a couple of conservation-minded couplets, along with the "tin to win" fine print. Reprinted with permission of Campbell Soup Co.

Copy Appeal	No. of Ads	Percent
Increasing war plan production	313	30
Selling War Bonds	172	16.6
Conservation of time, material, foodstuffs	149	14.4
Improving national health	97	9.4
Improving labor relations	38	3.7
Promoting salvage campaigns	34	3.3
Preventing sabotage	7	.7
Explaining price control	7	.7
Miscellaneous wartime ads	132	12.7
Grand total	949	91.5

At the time of this exhibit, the sale of war bonds ranked second as a theme, but it soon took over first place, because the Treasury Department was a colossus of ads, posters, and other creative appeals during the

ILLUSTRATION FROM WALT DISNEY'S PRODUCTION, "VICTORY THROUGH AIRPOW

Blast the hub and smash the wheel!

LOOK TO *Lockheed* FOR LEADERSHIP

LOCKHEED AIRCRAFT CORPORATION · BURBANK, CALIFORNIA

Many trade groups banded together to issue institutional advertising in support of the war effort and other more parochial goals. The mention of "arbitrarily limit" implies some unspecified government intervention, common during the war. Bataan was an attention-getter, since it (and Corregidor) symbolized the loss of the Philippines in March and April of 1942. Thousands of captured American and Filipino troops died or were executed on the ensuing 65–mile march through the jungle.

war. Between May 1, 1941, and June 30, 1945, Americans were persuaded to buy nearly $46 billion worth of E bonds. Although the bonds could be cashed in just 60 days, only $7 billion worth were redeemed during the war. The payroll deduction plan, heavily pitched in Treasury Department ads, sold $485 million worth of bonds to 25 million people in just one month (April 1945). "Citizens were solemnly told that unless they bought bonds more Americans would be killed, which was absurdly untrue," wrote Henry Pringle in his essay for *While You Were Gone.* "A safe assumption is that most Americans bought bonds because they were an excellent investment, a hedge against post-war depression, and because they felt a patriotic compulsion to do so."

Another branch of the government, the military services, also readily advertised. An army general declared that "advertising is one of the most powerful weapons in our armament." In 1943, an advertising executive rhetorically asked, "What's all this pother about whether the government should advertise? It already is advertising, extensively. Those sensible fellows who run the Army and Navy make no bones about it, and seem to have no difficulties over it."

These disparate elements—the shortage of commercial goods, the vigor of federal drum-beating, and the intensity of volunteer and public-interest efforts to aid the war—rewrote and redrew advertising in America. "Taken as a whole, the advertising of 1943 is something new under the sun," wrote Kenneth Davis, a Commerce Department analyst. "It has been just as much converted as has the sewing machine plant that now turns out machine guns. . . . The customary role of a seller of products had to be generally abandoned, and a new one—as a seller of ideas—adopted."

Ads could sell ideas in several ways, as illustrated by a letter that the Treasury Department sent to both radio and print advertisers, asking them to support the war bond "Minute Man" campaign in one of three ways: At a minimum, run the Minute Man insignia with a one-line request. Or the ad could feature a box containing a "brief sales message" about the war bonds. Or, the third and largest option, a full ad in which war bond

material was "either the dominant theme or an integral part of the ad itself."

Near the lower end of the spectrum of donated space is an ad for Roma wines; in tiny type, it says, "before you buy wines—buy War Bonds and Stamps."

The war effort altered the content and the tone of ads in several ways. Instead of what one analyst called "dramatic lay-outs and sophisticated copy" of the pre-war ads, a short description of illustrated shoes appeared in one series of ads from a shoe manufacturer. Instead of pre-war ads that mentioned "shoes that are fraught with daring," the wartime text said, "tailored to a custom-made trimness for duty and daytime."

Ads for many of the remaining commercial products certainly became more practical. One ad man wrote of an experience he had in August 1943, when he looked at the cabbages growing in his garden and then noticed an ad for Morton's salt that offered a booklet

about how to make sauerkraut. "Now that's what I call intelligent wartime advertising—good for me, good for the country, and good for the advertiser," he wrote.

Once a company decided to continue advertising, it had to figure out what sort of ads to create. Radical changes were necessary, particularly for those companies no longer making civilian goods for the duration of the war. Instead of writing about the glorious acceleration of that 1940 Ford V–8, for example, copywriters were describing U-boat strafings. Instead of drawing happy couples making "goo-goo eyes" at their lush new carpet or a grinning husband snatching bacon from a platter held by his wife, artists were drawing soldiers slogging through a jungle.

An ad for Pepperell Manufacturing Company showed a hospital scene with a nurse taking a patient's temperature. A uniformed man sits at the bedside. "Can anything else matter?" the headline asks. "*Your* sheets can wait," the copy says. "Somewhere there's a bed like this that needs them. It must have them before you get yours. Nothing else matters so much today to you or to us. Victory is *Everybody's* business," it concludes.

The promotional efforts by the Commerce Department were just one element in the frantic economic landscape. As a result, members of the advertising industry were still confused about the overall plan of attack. Would the government restrict the content of advertising or prohibit it altogether? Would it buy its own advertising, or pay for that section of commercial ads dedicated to civilian or military themes? Gradually, the answers were clarified. In late 1942, one advertising executive wrote, "the situation with regard to the government use of advertising seems to be clarifying itself, thanks to the joint efforts of OWI [the Office of War Information] and the Advertising Council. There are big jobs to be done. . . . no agency man who isn't drafted will need to go looking for war work."

One problem that quickly cropped up was rationing of paper, both magazine stock and newsprint. Publishers in general received allocations that were cut about 10 percent compared to their usage during the previous year. "The effect on advertising has been most apparent in magazines," wrote Kenneth Davis in May 1943. "Many publishers have now accepted all of the

MAINTAIN YOUR GOODWILL

Brand goodwill is a capital asset of almost unlimited value: difficult to build: only too easy to lose

ADVERTISE AS USUAL

ISSUED BY THE ADVERTISING ASSOCIATION

At the outset of war, faced with shortages of paper and civilian products, many people questioned whether advertising was even necessary. The question had already been asked in England; the answer appeared in this British ad, and the same answer became widely accepted in the United States.

business they can handle for the remainder of the year," a problem many businessmen would love to have more often. "In some cases publishers have found it necessary to ration the space available."

In a public relations effort to make sure that publications got their share of paper, the National Publishers Association issued the pamphlet *Magazines and the War*, touting the role of print media: "To weld the impregnable American will power is the special job of our psychological forces. It must be done by national magazines, newspapers and radio. Like members of a bomber's crew, these forces are highly specialized.

Next page
Combat boots came to symbolize the soldier during the war, appearing in dozens of ads as visual shorthand for the combat experience and for the boys "over there." The ad appeared in May 1944.

PUT YOURSELF IN HIS SHOES

What would YOU expect of the folks back home?

It has been a long time since these feet touched the soil of the U. S. A. It may be still longer before they are turned toward home again. They are on a bitter road that must be followed to an unknown end.

And above these feet, in their muddy shoes, is a man who loves life, its comforts and its pleasures as much as you and I. But he is willing to sacrifice all for us.

What are we giving up for him?

We cannot share his hardships. We cannot share his danger. But we can back him up with the finest equipment. And we also can make sure that he won't have to face the evils of inflation when he comes back home.

We can do all this simply by digging deep into our pay for more War Bonds —more than we think we can afford to buy. And after we have bought them, we can hold on to them by sacrificing some of our luxuries and comforts.

That's no more than our plain, clear duty to our fighting men, to our country, and to ourselves. *Let's show the world we know how to do it!* Belmont Radio Corporation, 5923 West Dickens Avenue, Chicago 39, Illinois.

Belmont Radio
TELEVISION ★ FM ★ ELECTRONICS

★ *LET'S ALL BACK THE ATTACK WITH WAR BONDS* ★

Success depends upon enabling each to function to the utmost"—in other words, give them plenty of paper.

An equally serious problem involved personnel: "Publishers and broadcasters feel that the most serious problem with which they have to contend is that of manpower," Davis added. "Although both industries are classified as essential, many of their employees not in key positions have been drafted."

Paper shortages were much more severe in England, where newspapers became four-page bulletins, ads were cut to the bone, and the government became the single largest advertiser, paying its own way.

Although tempting, it is misleading to ascribe oversimplified motives to human behavior. That statement certainly holds true for wartime advertising. Unsullied patriotism may have been the predominant element among the reasons that the war took over the content of many ads, but it certainly wasn't the only reason.

War or no war, manufacturers are always anxious to keep their brand names visible. The 1948 Colgate-Palmolive annual report explained, "During the war, supplies were limited due to shortages of raw materials and packaging materials. Consumers were often unable to buy their usual or favorite brands. Instead they had to accept products with which they were unfamiliar. During this shortage period many brands were advertised consistently in order to keep their names and merits before the public. . . . When free markets returned, in practically every classification, advertised brands came back in stronger than before."

Kenneth Davis wrote, "Many advertisers whose products are off the market for the duration of the war are devoting their efforts to keeping alive brand names that were worth millions to their owners before the war." A businessman didn't have to have a long white beard to remember what happened during World War I, when the companies that made some nationally known products simply stopped advertising, and "were never able to recapture the markets they gave up during wartime."

Within the ad industry, the basic issues had been clear before Pearl Harbor. An article in the June 1941 edition of the *Ayer News Files* said, "One of the most important jobs facing America's major industries in the present emergency is an informative job—telling the public the contributions they are making to national defense, keeping the name and reputation of the products and services fresh in the public mind, preserving the good name of business and proving the advantages of the democratic system."

"Wartime Advertising Serves As Well As Sells," read one headline in *Advertising and Its Role in War and Peace.* The article, reprinted from the April 1, 1943 issue of *Domestic Commerce,* described several specific reasons that the continuation of advertising was necessary. First, the necessity of "keeping brand names and trademarks alive regardless of whether a product is available or not." The article recalled several instances from World War I—products such as Pear's Soap, Force Breakfast Food, and Sweet Caporal cigarettes—

in which companies' advertising "dropped from sight," and they ended up discovering "just how forgetful is the public."

Manufacturers that were only doing war work developed "good will" advertising and stressed a variety of war-related and brand-related themes. And, as Donald Nelson, head of the WPB, pointed out, most of this advertising was tax-deductible.

As early as 1942, even before the United States declared war, advertising analysts and planners were looking to the postwar era for reasons to continue commercial ads during the conflict. "All of us will face piled-up wants when this war is over and we have given up at last the necessity of doing without," one speaker told those attending a Florida Chamber of Commerce meeting. "Today our productive genius is bending every ounce of effort to winning the war. But in the very act of doing this, new discoveries are being made . . . discoveries that can be transformed quickly into goods of peace."

"Nevertheless," the pep talk continued, "demand will have to be stimulated. A wanting public, heaped high with lacks, will need to be informed." The payoff for wartime advertising will come during peacetime, when "you will have laid the ground work for a flow of

Next page
This ad's mention of the company's experience in wartime production is apt. During World War I, the Winchester Repeating Arms Company began its war-related production in 1914, when it sold 50 million .22-caliber cartridges to the British, and contracted to make 100,000 Model 95 rifles for the Russians. During World War I, Winchester produced Browning automatic rifles, bayonets, mortar shells, and cartridges. The company again began making rifles (semi-automatic Garands) for the military in 1936; it had contracted for (and begun delivering) 65,000 of them in 1940. The company would end up producing 513,582 of them. Its first order specifically for World War II, however, was from Finland, which needed ammunition. The company received an order for 350,000 .30-caliber M1 rifles in November 1941, and would eventually produce 818,000 of them. On Jan. 13, 1942, Winchester stopped all commercial manufacturing. Among its totals for World War II production were 15.2 billion cartridges and 1,440,000 firearms, along with aircraft radiator tubes, batteries, and 162 million targets. Courtesy, Olin Corp.

Page 119
A series of ads from the Florida Citrus Commission, of which this May 1944 ad is a good example, were full of illustrations, themes, logos, and slogans. By early 1943, the Commission reported that "Shipments to the military had become 'regular' . . . the Quartermaster Market Center, Tampa, had purchased in a three-week period 250 cars of fresh citrus fruit." Citrus products were deemed so important that in January 1944, canners were notified that they would receive more tinplate to use in canning blended and orange juice, most of which (this ad points out) went to the military. Courtesy, State of Florida Department of Citrus

"It's Messerschmitts not Mallards today, Bill!"

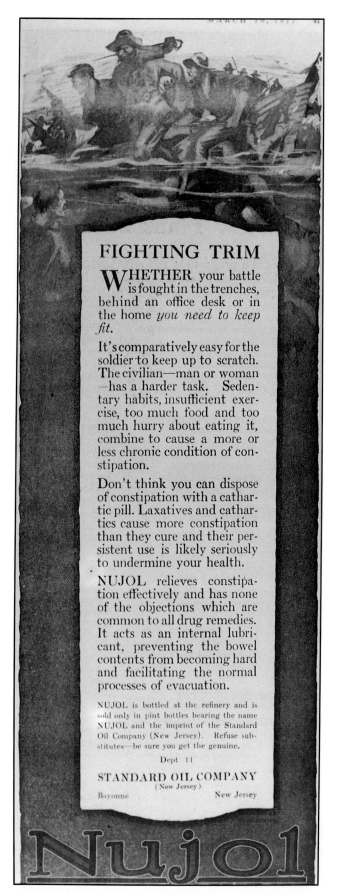

FIGHTING TRIM

WHETHER your battle is fought in the trenches, behind an office desk or in the home *you need to keep fit.*

It's comparatively easy for the soldier to keep up to scratch. The civilian—man or woman—has a harder task. Sedentary habits, insufficient exercise, too much food and too much hurry about eating it, combine to cause a more or less chronic condition of constipation.

Don't think you can dispose of constipation with a cathartic pill. Laxatives and cathartics cause more constipation than they cure and their persistent use is likely seriously to undermine your health.

NUJOL relieves constipation effectively and has none of the objections which are common to all drug remedies. It acts as an internal lubricant, preventing the bowel contents from becoming hard and facilitating the normal processes of evacuation.

NUJOL is bottled at the refinery and is sold only in pint bottles bearing the name NUJOL and the imprint of the Standard Oil Company (New Jersey). Refuse substitutes—be sure you get the genuine.

Dept 11

STANDARD OIL COMPANY
(New Jersey)
Bayonne   New Jersey

orders when the floodgates of a pent-up purchasing power are opened."

As Raymond Rubicam wrote after the war in his essay for the book *While You Were Gone*, "Advertising's role in the war was a minor one, no matter how you stretch it, but advertising's role in peace would be major." Society could create jobs, but the demand for the goods produced by those jobs had to be there or the result would be pointless. "Mass demand does not exist unaided," he wrote.

These two convincing reasons—brand familiarity and postwar planning—were based on economic realities. Neither had much to do with patriotism, except for the fact that if the United States lost the war, all bets were off. Nevertheless, the question of whether advertising was necessary boiled up into quite a controversy early in the war. "One frequently voiced public reaction has been—'Why not save paper through cutting down advertising?'" wrote a government spokesman in the April 1943 issue of *Domestic Commerce*. "Others ask—'Why not cut out all advertising by companies who have nothing to sell?'" An official from the Commerce Department wrote, "There are those who shortsightedly view it as an economic waste of time. The Government as a whole strongly disagrees with this attitude. In writings and in public utterances President Roosevelt and other officials have gone on record as favoring advertising. They have heartily endorsed its wartime role."

During the war, people were hungry for news, as evidenced by increases in newspaper and magazine circulations and in the number of radio listeners. The news media and the entertainment media were often one and the same, and they had to support what one writer described as "an elaborate, far-flung system of news gathering." Advertising revenue paid most of the bill. Most of the time, he pointed out, "magazines subsist and prosper on advertising . . . advertisers 'pay the freight' for the fiction, the illustrations, the serious articles."

Although American industry seemed to have the most tangible and quantifiable role in the homefront war effort, countless other purely civilian groups and organizations played specific, important roles. The media were inseparably involved, as were advertising agencies, which organized themselves into a group that was first called the Advertising Council and then by the more familiar War Advertising Council (WAC).

The techniques of advertising during World War I scarcely changed, although many writers, artists, and executives volunteered to help George Creel, who was

Advertising during World War I continued almost unchanged, although many ad writers, artists, and executives volunteered to help George Creel, head of government information. Unlike during World War II, there was no organized effort of the advertising industry. This March 1917 ad was an exception to the rule, although the connection between combat and constipation was murky.

120

head of the Committee on Public Information (CPI), the government's information office. They organized themselves into the National War Advisory Board, helping the government with fund-raising and recruiting, and were eventually "incorporated" as the Division of Advertising in the CPI. They sold war bonds, worked to "enhance worker morale," and promoted conservation of food and resources. They produced some emotionally powerful ads, and the war bond campaigns were quite successful. Manufacturers and publishers donated $2.5 million worth of ad space in 1918, about 1.5 percent of the total for that year.

In retrospect, that would seem a pittance. During World War II, the WAC involved thousands of advertisers and media outlets and hundreds of agencies, all as volunteers. Its goals were to make advertising "useful" during the war, to plan and organize the overall ad campaign, and to persuade people and firms to donate space, time, and talent to "hammer home to the people by all available means the points which the government selected as being most important to the war," Rubicam wrote in his synopsis of the effort.

The WAC often teamed up with other federal agencies. For instance, the credit on an informational package about the Sixth War Loan read, "Prepared by War Finance Division, Treasury Department, and Domestic Branch, Office of War Information, in cooperation with War Advertising Council."

A volunteer advertising committee for the National War Fund, organized through the WAC, prepared in a typical year 18,000 portfolios containing proofsheets on approximately seventy advertisements for national and local use, ranging in size from full-page to single-column.

In *Mobilizing Women for War*, Leila Rupp wrote that, thanks to the WAC, "a barrage of advertising descended on the advertisers themselves, urging them to devote all or half of each ad to government themes, or to work war themes into advertising copy."

Many ads took on semi-official overtones which today seem odd. An ad for V–8 juice, for example, has a rectangular inset at the top right which says, in block letters:

U.S. NEEDS US STRONG
VEGETABLE JUICES
THIS TYPE OF FOOD
IS AMONG THOSE
RECOMMENDED IN THE
NUTRITION FOOD RULES
EAT NUTRITIONAL FOOD

A small credit line at the bottom of this panel says, "Reproduced by permission only, Office of Defense Health and Welfare Services."

The chairman of the WAC was Chester J. La Roche, who worked closely with Donald Nelson. A national shortage of scrap iron and steel was an immediate, pressing problem when the WAC went to work, but the Treasury Department's payroll-deduction war bond drive became its first "client." The WAC later

Glossy hopes and promises about what would happen after the war became common in 1944 and 1945. This General Electric ad is among the earliest ones that looked beyond the war; when it appeared in March 1943, the "untold comforts and conveniences" must have seemed far off indeed to the average consumer, who was just coming to grips with rationing and shortages. Courtesy, The General Electric Hall of History Foundation

coordinated drives for scrap and fat salvage, in which companies or industries sponsored the campaigns. In many cases, companies devoted part of their regular ads to government themes, an approach that the WAC would find the most productive.

The WAC was unquestionably successful, and it carefully tabulated its contributions after the war. In 1942, the WAC coordinated fourteen informational

Next page
This November 1942 ad typifies those produced by companies no longer making commercial products for the duration of the war. The portfolio was a logical offer: By the end of 1944, 85 million Americans owned war bonds, in part due to the massive federal ad campaign promoting their sale. The Fifth War Loan, the largest one of the series, deluged the public with more than 200,000 ads, selling $27 billion worth of bonds. Courtesy, Borg-Warner Corp.

Keep Your War Bonds in this
FREE BUDGET PORTFOLIO

Budget each bond for a specific after-war use

As a service to America's patriotic War Bond buyers, Norge offers this useful War Bond Budget Portfolio free on request. It serves you as a convenient container for bonds—as a guard against misplacing them—as a systematic method of budgeting each bond for later use. Half the pleasure in life lies in planning for the future. This Portfolio provides the ideal method for planning and achieving your goal.

Buy more War Bonds regularly for Victory—and budget them in the Portfolio bond compartments for savings, children's education, travel and vacation, new house or farm, new car or plane. The complete, compact Portfolio will hold and budget up to 100 U. S. War Bonds. ☆ Send for your free Budget Portfolio. Write today to Department 2, Norge Division, Borg-Warner Corporation, Detroit, Michigan.

★ ★ ★

The entire resources of Norge are devoted to war production. Norge believes it can make an additional contribution toward Victory by offering this practical Budget Portfolio free to all War Bond buyers. Be patriotic—buy more War Bonds to win the war. Be wise—budget them for Tomorrow's use. And this Christmas—give War Bonds. Present them in this free Portfolio. Write for your free Portfolio now. This offer expires February 20, 1943.

WHEN WE WIN—SEE NORGE BEFORE YOU BUY

NORGE
HOUSEHOLD APPLIANCES

NORGE DIVISION · BORG-WARNER CORPORATION · DETROIT · MICHIGAN

campaigns for eight federal agencies, producing $150 million in donated ad space and radio time. By 1944, the numbers had risen to sixty-two drives for twenty-seven agencies and $302 million. Topics included scrap metal and fat salvage; curbing absenteeism; recruiting women for the military; victory gardens; food conservation; fuel, tin can, and rubber conservation; Red Cross drives; and, biggest of all, war financing, which at one point even put its message onto diaper wrappers. Other special campaigns urged people to use V-mail to get more letters to servicemen, to avoid black market gas, and to curtail their holiday travel plans.

As is the case with most other things that people thought and did during the war, there were tensions and controversies. Some people thought that the government should pay for all non-commercial advertising. Others mistrusted business in general, looking for non-patriotic, hidden commercial motives (at worst, a sort of Daddy Warbucks-style profiteering). Still others thought the "soap salesmen" would botch their handling of war themes (a fear that was justified in some cases).

Within advertising, some people "gagged at the thought of working, in effect, for Franklin Roosevelt," wrote Stephen Fox in *The Mirror Makers*. "Outside advertising, some insisted that writers and journalists, not advertising men, should speak for the government in wartime."

Early in the war, some advertisers feared that the Treasury Department would deny advertising as an allowable business expense during the war. But advertising kept its tax deduction—and, along with the rest of the economy, boomed.

To some extent, war-related advertising was riding the wartime surge of interest in all media. Since more people were buying more magazines and newspapers and listening to more radio stations, there were more vehicles for advertising. In 1942, Sunday papers registered their greatest circulation increase for any one year, a gain of three million readers. Magazines also showed sizeable growth that year, selling more than 185 million copies.

By the end of the war, the WAC and its federal clients had quite a success story to tell. For just one campaign, more than 135,000 posters and bulletins about war bonds were created and distributed, with space valued at $2,225,000 and reaching an audience of 51,500,000 people. Treasury Department officials had tabulated approximately $26 million in donated advertisements per year. Newspapers donated nearly 19,000 full pages of news and editorial space to publicizing the Fifth War Loan, almost a quarter of which was on front pages. Some 4,000 daily and weekly newspapers printed a facsimile of a $100 war bond on the drive's opening day, amid headlines such as "Hero's Mother Aids Bond Sale" and "Pilot, Prisoner in Germany, Invests in Seven $100 Bonds."

OWI director Elmer Davis estimated that the newspaper and magazine space of food advertisers who adapted their copy to government campaigns was valued at more than $16 million in 1943.

The success of specific campaigns has been well documented. By the end of 1944, 85 million Americans owned war bonds, thanks in part to $400 million worth of donated time and space, with individual ads numbering in the millions. Some 65,291 women were recruited to the Cadet Nurse Corps, 40 percent of them by one series of magazine advertisements. By 1944, 18 million victory gardens had been planted, producing nearly two-fifths of the fresh produce consumed by civilians.

Sources put the ultimate total of donated advertising at between several hundred million and a billion dollars' worth of space and time.

The WAC had certainly earned its share of kudos. A typical one came from Secretary of the Treasury Henry Morgenthau, Jr., who said, "The Treasury Department is keenly aware of the really magnificent contribution both advertisers and advertising agencies have made and are making to the success of the Second War Loan. In any voluntary, cooperative effort such as this, requiring the cooperation of all America, the advertising profession has always played a leading role. In the Second War Loan, that role has been a magnificent and inspiring one to us all."

Other assessments were more measured and, as a result, more moving. Raymond Rubicam wrote, "The devotion of advertising to the war had been as inconsistent as the devotion of civilians. Some had given much, others nothing. . . . But no nation ever gave so much to a war in which the fighting was so far away— and gave so largely by voluntary action of its people."

"BEAR DOWN, MISTER... BEAR DOWN!"

I don't have to look at her ...

I don't have to watch my ship die ...

All my life long I'll see her in my mind's eye ...

And always I'll hear the high, faint roar of planes circling ... circling ... circling ... as their gas runs low and they've nowhere to go and the guys at the sticks look down and tears spill over the lids of their eyes and they stiffen their lips.

Ever lose *your* ship, Mister?

Ever lose your mother?

Ever lose your girl?

Your heart cracks and the weight on your back seems to push you under and you think you'll drown, but you don't.

You carry on, not for yourself but for the rest of the folks ... for the family ... the kids ... for guys like these swimming around, circling around with night coming on and no ship to come home to and around and below only the empty sea.

But we don't want pity!

We'll come through! ... We'll find another ship! ... We'll get back! ... because we're *free* men, born to be on our own ... brought up to fight on a team or alone ... trained to *live* for our country, not to give up and die!

So, bear down, Mister ... bear down ...

For every drop of blood they spill ... for every heart they break ... for every tear that's shed ... for every ship that's sunk ... for every plane it costs ... for every man of ours who's lost ... they'll pay with ten of their own!

Bear down, Mister ... bear down ..:

So the freedom we want ...

So the futures we want ...

So the country we want ...

Will be there when we get back!

• • •

Here at Nash-Kelvinator we're building Pratt & Whitney engines for the Navy's Vought Corsairs and Grumman Hellcats ... Hamilton Standard propellers for United Nations bombers ... governors, binoculars, parts for ships, jeeps, tanks and trucks ... readying production lines for Sikorsky helicopters. All of us devoted 100% to winning this war ... to speeding the peace when our men will come back to their jobs and homes and even better futures than they had before ... to the day when we'll build for you an even finer Kelvinator, an even greater Nash!

NASH-KELVINATOR CORPORATION
Kenosha · Milwaukee · DETROIT · Grand Rapids · Lansing

NASH
AUTOMOBILES
KELVINATOR
REFRIGERATORS · ELECTRIC RANGES

Chapter 5

Censorship And The Office Of War Information

"Hello, Central, Give Me No-Man's-Land"

Anyone with a basic knowledge of the realities of combat quickly recognizes that ads offer a selective portrait of war. Advertising isn't the same as investigative reporting, much less routine journalism.

There is no single type of war-related ad. They range from the bluntly realistic to the serious, informative, and no-nonsense, to the upbeat, corny, and wouldn't-it-be-nice-to-think-so varieties, in which the war tends to be clean, wholesome, and almost attractive.

In his book *Wartime*, Paul Fussell compares this latter view of the war with "the artificially cheerful servicemen's faces displayed in framed pictures in wartime living rooms. From those pictures you'd get the impression that being in the war was really rather jolly, everyone's so smiling and jaunty."

Advertisements are one facet of the spectrum of what passes for information during a war. Looking for truth in advertising is a puzzling business at best, especially during wartime, when there are so many conflicting and incomplete versions of the truth floating around, and when the government is largely in control of the official version. Sen. Hiram Johnson's famous quote from 1917 applies: "The first casualty when war comes is truth."

Lots of messages were floating around during World War II. People were intensely hungry for news of the war; the amount of radio time spent by NBC (National Broadcasting Company) on news rose from 6.3 percent in 1939 to 15.4 percent in 1942. That year, a March ad for NBC pictured a soldier holding crutches

and talking into a microphone. "To our armed forces, NBC is a two-way tie," the copy said. "For people at home it provides the 'Army Hour'—weekly presentation of the War Department . . . a personalized saga generally conceded to be one of radio's greatest wartime contributions." In 1944, the amount of time devoted to news climbed to 20.4 percent.

Folks were also hungry for entertainment, and there were more and more media vehicles for both. Circulation boomed for all forms of print media. Newspaper sales in 1942 were up more than 2 million for a total of 44 million per day, and the sale of Sunday papers was up more than 3 million compared to the previous year. Magazine readership rose even more: Nearly 27 million more copies were sold in 1942 than in 1941, a total of more than 185 million copies.

In 1944, more than 200 million words from more than 500 war correspondents were sent from the fighting fronts to stateside newspapers. According the pamphlet *Magazines and the War* issued by the National Publishers Association, by January 1943, national magazines had printed 1,500 stories about the war, nearly 3,800 pages worth. "Take any issue and about fifty percent of the editorial material is pictures, articles and other contributions to victorious public opinion," it said.

These "contributions" added to the murky stew of advertising images, censored letters and news releases, gossip, and rumor. In spite of this, though, most people ended up with a fairly realistic view of the war.

Early in the war, the glut of "news" became apparent to planners in Washington, who feared that the

Previous page
Late in the war, Nash-Kelvinator launched a memorable series of ads featuring realistic illustrations and gritty, no-nonsense prose, usually in a first-person format. The copy was superbly written, if a bit dramatic, and the ads managed to avoid over-glamorizing the soldier's job. The April 1944 entry underlined the grim casualties of war. Courtesy, White Consolidated Industries, Inc.

Next page
Just when you think that ads are safe and comfortable, you discover moments of horror: "the air will suck out and their lungs will burst . . . row on row how white the crosses grow." The artist for the illustration got to sign his name, but the author of the text is, unfortunately, unknown. Courtesy, White Consolidated Industries, Inc.

"I'LL COME THROUGH..."

They hate me . . .

They're afraid of me . . .

They've got to get me . . .

Penned up in their pillbox, they know if I get to a gun slit alive, I'll shove the nozzle inside and turn on the heat and the air will suck out and their lungs will burst and their will to fight will go up in a roaring flame.

Creeping along . . . crawling along . . . inching along . . .

While the sweat trickles down from your arm-pits and ice water runs down your spine and your guts pull in as the guns begin . . . and the bullets cut ruts in the rock where you're going to be and where you've just been . . .

You think of the strangest things . . .

The way Bill smiled when he won a pot . . . how Jack hoped for a letter he never got . . . and row on row how white the crosses grow. And it all runs together with pictures of home . . . like that day in the ninth when you went to bat with two out and two on . . . and they asked for a hit and you came through in the pinch and you won.

I'll come through again . . .

I know I'll come through because I've got to. Because in the Marines a man is trained to stand alone . . . trained to work, to dare, to take a chance, to go ahead on his own . . . not just for himself but his buddy, his platoon, his regiment, the Corps . . . his wife . . . his kids . . . the country he's willing to fight and die for.

That's the spirit that made America strong . . .

That's the spirit that's going to win this war . . .

That's what I'll be looking for when I come home.

Here at Nash-Kelvinator we're building Pratt & Whitney engines for the Navy's Vought Corsairs and Grumman Hellcats . . . Hamilton Standard propellers for United Nations bombers . . . governors, binoculars, parts for ships, jeeps, tanks and trucks . . . readying production lines for Sikorsky helicopters. All of us devoted 100% to winning this war . . . to speeding the peace when our men will come back to their jobs and homes and even better futures than they had before . . . to the day when we'll build for you an even finer Kelvinator, an even greater Nash!

The Army-Navy "E" awarded to Nash-Kelvinator Corp., Propeller Division.

NASH-KELVINATOR CORPORATION
Kenosha · Milwaukee · DETROIT · Grand Rapids · Lansing

LET'S ALL BACK THE ATTACK!
BUY EXTRA WAR BONDS.

NASH
AUTOMOBILES
KELVINATOR
REFRIGERATORS · ELECTRIC RANGES

public was in danger of becoming stupefied by it all. Information poured in daily from the combat fronts, foreign capitols, regional federal offices, and Washington, DC, itself. The Office of Facts and Figures had already issued the *Radio War Guide* that steered broadcasters toward targeting a few government programs or campaigns a week, instead of issuing wholesale barrages.

What the government needed, the planners figured, was what one historian called "a new superpress bureau." As a result, the Office of Facts and Figures (along with the Office of Government Reports, and the Division of Information of the Office for Emergency Management) were absorbed into the Office of War Information (OWI), which would play a huge role in shaping the content of wartime ads. According to historian Geoffrey Perrett, the OWI was created on June 13, 1942 "to take charge of domestic propaganda and, in effect, sell the war." Until its official termination on September 15, 1945, the OWI cleared and coordinated releases of information from government sources, trying to prevent conflicting reports. By March 1943, the OWI's news bureau was issuing 250 news releases a week to 1,867 daily papers, which had a total circulation of 41.4 million.

For radio, the OWI developed a system for using the time and personnel donated by radio stations and program sponsors. It coordinated the use of newspaper and advertising space and radio time donated to the government to carry advertising on its war-information campaigns.

Speaking to the New York State Publishers Association on September 14, 1943, OWI director Elmer Davis declared, "Every newspaper in this country is an office of war information—and every radio station, every magazine, every book publisher, every motion picture company. . . ."

The OWI could look to its British counterpart—the Ministry of Information (MOI), later (in 1945) the Central Office of Information—for precedent. Via the MOI, the British government "became the greatest patron of commercial art and literature that the advertising business had ever known," wrote George Begley in *Keep Mum! Advertising Goes to War.*

In America, the OWI was both influential and controversial. Critics called it "a swarm of advertising men" who were "happily painting the war in glowing terms." According to Thomas Stokes in his essay for *While You Were Gone,* the OWI was "almost as unpopular with some in Congress" as the Office of Price Administration because political opponents of President Roosevelt thought that it favored the administration. "This information and propaganda agency was the subject of almost ceaseless investigation," Stokes wrote immediately after the war. In *Mobilizing Women for War,* Leila Rupp noted that the OWI's domestic branch "soon ran into trouble" because the writers and the advertising executives were at odds. "The writers wanted simply to inform the people and disapproved of the Madison Avenue approach employed by the advertising personnel," Rupp wrote. Writers and researchers resigned in mass in April 1943, issuing a statement to the press in which they complained that the OWI's domestic branch was run by "high-pressure promoters who prefer slick salesmanship to honest information." That year, Congress sharply curtailed activities of the OWI's domestic branch; the foreign branch, which managed propaganda in enemy and neutral countries, survived unscathed.

Nevertheless, the OWI effectively accomplished the government's goals, exerting a tangible influence on the topics covered by the media. Although its budget was $9 million in 1944, its effect was many times that. In *Advertising and Its Role in War and Peace,* a book published a year earlier by the Department of Commerce, Elmer Davis wrote, "The press, radio, magazines, motion pictures, and advertisers of America have gladly spent many hundreds of millions of dollars to carry war information to the American people."

In a nutshell, the OWI's job was to get folks fired up beforehand and congratulate them afterwards. It didn't stint on purple prose, as evidenced by an informational package about the Fifth War Loan: "As American tanks tore into Brittany and swerved toward Paris . . . as the Russians knifed through to the Baltic in Latvia and knocked with thunder at the gates of Warsaw . . . as the Stars and Stripes flew again over Guam . . . the nation at home had kept pace. On the road to victory, the American people had taken their fifth mighty step."

By 1943, the OWI had helped set up the Writers' War Board (WWB), whose central organizer was mystery writer Rex Stout, author of the Nero Wolfe stories. The WWB would be a full-time job for him during the war. It functioned as a private organization assisting the government; one writer called it a "volunteer extension."

"Government spokesmen rarely went beyond requests and suggestions," Stout said, denying that there was any government control of the WWB's activities. The WWB, which would grow to 5,000 volunteers at its peak, started by helping the Treasury Department enlist writers for war bond campaigns. Members also wrote songs, radio scripts, pulp-magazine articles, speeches, jingles, slogans, and news fillers.

The combined effects of the OWI and the WWB were felt in many ways apart from advertising. In magazine serials, the heroes and heroines began discussing aspects of the war. The authors of nonfiction books and articles volunteered to write pamphlets and books about war-related themes. Script writers for both radio and film took on similar tasks. The OWI and the War Activities Committee of the motion picture industry collaborated on a ten-minute film for the National War Fund, which was shown in 13,000 movie houses and would be updated annually.

At the end of their shows, even comedians would give "eloquent and sincere" talks about what Norman Corwin described as "war subjects allocated by the

"I was a Prisoner of War"

IN LETTERS from liberated prisoners of war and internees—from their families—in personal visits to Kraft offices all over the country—the story of Kraft Products in the war continues to come in. It is a story too big to ever fit into words. The letters alone, if quoted in full, would fill several issues of The Kraftsman.

Yet it is a story that every Kraft worker should have the privilege of knowing. It's good to know that something we have done has helped, even a little. It's good to know that we can be proud of the quality of Kraft products, as they proved themselves in the test of war.

It's good, too, to think about a lesson these letter writers and visitors can teach us. They learned it the very hard way. It's a lesson of appreciation of the many good things we have—of complaining less about the things we cannot get. The appreciation of these men and women is sincere and great enough to cause them to offer their tributes entirely unsolicited.

Here, then, are some "samples" of what they say. The Kraftsman passes on their thanks to the thousands of Kraft men and women all over the country, whose untiring efforts kept the supply of Kraft products moving out to those who needed them most.

From a Spokane, Wash. Staff Sergeant:

"What I want to say is: 'Thanks a million for a can of butter'. You see, I was a Japanese prisoner of war for 40 months, and believe me, food was scarce over there.

"So when the Red Cross got food parcels through to us, you can imagine how we felt. Today, when my buddy asked me what I liked best out of the

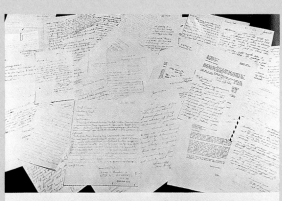

"I was a Prisoner of War"

Nothing brought the fortunes of war home more vividly than letters from prisoners. The Kraft employee newsletter printed a special feature of dozens of letters from former employees. Courtesy, Kraft General Foods, Inc.

food packages, right away without hesitation I said: 'I guess it was the cheesey Kraft Spread, which tasted so good in coffee and on crackers'.

"It took over a year to get to us, but tasted and was as fresh as the day it was packed. So thanks again for a wonderful product which came well timed, as we sure needed it."

From an Albuquerque, N. M. Captain in the Army:

"I was captured by the Japs on April 9, 1942, and made a prisoner of war, with the fall of Bataan. Food was very short. How we survived on the 1200 to 1500 calories of food we received daily, I'll never know.

"In November, 1944, everyone in camp was at a very low ebb, physically and mentally. At that time we received Red Cross boxes. In each box, among other things, were 3 or 4 cans of your Army Spread and one-half pound of your cheese—two very important things. First, your particular cheese was never spoiled. Second, the butter or Army Spread was always to everyone in camp the most important item in the box and it was up against some good ones—like chocolate, jam, raisins, cigarets, etc. I know, for I always traded the other items for the butter. I usually sat down, opened a can, and ate it with a spoon, like you would ice cream.

"I would like to shake your hand and thank you personally for everything you did to make a prisoner's life nearly human."

From the wife of a service man:

"My husband was a Prisoner of War in Germany. I sent him a parcel containing, among other articles of food, a box of Kraft Dinner. A year later this box was returned to us. Last week we ate that dinner. It was not only delicious, it had retained its flavor and freshness. Truly, a year's storage is a hard test on any product."

From a Seattle, Wash. BM 2/C, U. S. Navy:

"I wish to make known my appreciation, and I am sure that of hundreds of other prisoners of war. Having received foodstuff as a prisoner of war, through the Red Cross, in tropical climates of terrific heat, I want you to know that Kraft Cheese was always in perfect condition as the day packed.

"The fact was so well known among prisoners of war that it was every man's hope to get Kraft Cheese in his parcel, knowing he would have a good package of cheese to eat."

From an Elmhurst, Ill. Sergeant in the U. S. Marines:

"We were prisoners of war in the Far East, for the duration or thereabouts. During this time we received a few Red Cross food packages.

"In these packages, your cheese was a favorite among all. Excellent quality and in number one shape, always. You'd be surprised to know how many different ways it was prepared.

"We wish to extend our thanks, for all the boys who had the good fortune to receive a package with your product among its contents."

continued on next page

OWI." In *While You Were Gone,* Corwin quoted Eddie Cantor as saying, "Today, every comic has a serious note, whether it's for bonds or blood or conservation or tolerance."

Pro or con, gloomy or glad, the public was hungry for information about the war, and the government was anxious to feed it to them. As a Time, Incorporated, vice president wrote just after the war, every editor in the country felt compelled "to produce a wartime 'angle' for almost everything that went into print." The same could be said for most ads.

News of the war and its effects on the homefront permeated commercial media and employee newsletters alike. In its February-March 1942 issue, Kraft's *Cheesekraft* headlined one story, "Bataan Peninsula Men Ask For—And Get—Bing Crosby and KMH." The article said, "Out in the 'fox-holes of Bataan,' where General MacArthur and his gallant men are adding new lustre to the glories of American history, there came an hour's pause on Thursday night, January 29th. An hour's pause—and an hour of entertainment for the men fighting our battle in the far-off Philippines—as the Kraft Music Hall was transported, by short-wave radio, half a world away. . . ." The broadcast was made at the request of MacArthur and a colonel named Aken.

"Directly, simply, heart-warmingly, Bing talked to the men, sang favorite songs," it continued.

"Winnipeg Kraftman A Prisoner of War," another *Cheesekraft* article said, telling the story of a former employee who was an RCAF pilot and was shot down over Germany and held captive by the Nazis. The newsletter reprinted a postcard from the pilot. Throughout the war, the newsletter printed letters and pictures from former employees then in the service. "West Coast Kraftsmen Organize For Defense," another item reported. "Many of them devote three or four evenings a week to their training as air raid company commanders, sector wardens, and block wardens. Several are now serving on the Interceptor Squad of Civilian Air Raid defense. On call for any time of the night, they take their regular turn of three hours each as lookouts for enemy planes."

The May 1942 issue of *Cheesekraft* ran a photo of Kraft members of the California Women's Ambulance and Transport Corps, volunteer emergency workers trained in first aid, map reading, communications, and marksmanship. Another article was entitled "Kraft, England, Carries On With Vital Food Production After Two Years of War/Home Staff Redouble Efforts—Hayes Plant Continues Processing—Lend-Lease Food Receives Warm Welcome." A small item, datelined Denison, Texas, said, "Roy Coonrod left his job in the Kraft factory at Denison on December 9th to 'join up.' Roy's got one brother in the marines, one in the regular army . . . so he joined the Air Corps and is now being schooled as a mechanic."

Advertising was just one facet of the popular media, all of which were saturated with the sights, sounds, and ideas of the war. It would have been extremely odd if advertising had managed to ignore the war; nothing else did.

James Webb Young, author of *The Diary of an Ad Man,* complained about the quality and tone of the coverage early in the war: "How tired I am of all this tendency to ballyhoo the war," he wrote. "Magazine editors, newspapers columnists, radio commentators, and Washington headline hunters all seem determined to dramatize it and jazz it up. They act like press agents for a 'Roosevelt & Hopkins' Greatest Show on Earth.' It is true that for awhile we had ringside seats at history. But now we are in the ring, with a serious, dirty, and dangerous job to do. We ought to cut out the showmanship and get on with it."

Many of the central themes of the war and the media met, oddly enough, in the comic strips. Some cartoon characters joined right up—Skeezix Wallet of Frank King's *Gasoline Alley* and Terry of Milt Caniff's *Terry and the Pirates,* for example. In 1944, in fact, readers helped celebrate the marriage of Sgt. Skeezix Wallet to his boyhood sweetheart. Skeezix was home on furlough. Joe Palooka enlisted and stayed a private first class for the duration. Even in the funnies, the war was close and current.

Other popular strips, however—notably *Li'l Abner* and *Blondie*—ignored the war, on the assumption that folks turned to the comics for escape, not for reality. To some extent, that was true, as attested by letters home from GIs. Behind the scenes, the cartoonists who drew *Joe Palooka* (Ham Fisher) and *Li'l Abner* (Al Capp) were volunteering to create training manuals, pocket guides, language guides for invasion troops, and materials for war bond campaigns.

Whatever their stand on enlistment and war themes, the comics remained an extremely popular newspaper feature. Media experts had recognized the phenomenon for at least a decade. During a strike by newspaper deliverers in New York in 1945, readers were surveyed about what they missed most. They ranked comics in third place, behind general news and war news and ahead of editorials, sports, columns, and domestic news. Advertisements ranked sixth out of the twelve categories and was barely nosed out by sports (11.3 percent compared to 12 percent).

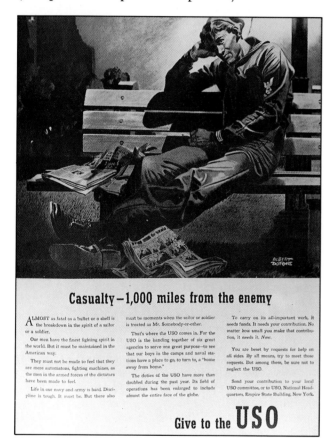

Casualty—1,000 miles from the enemy

A LMOST as fatal as a bullet or a shell is the breakdown in the spirit of a sailor or a soldier.

Our men have the finest fighting spirit in the world. But it must be maintained in the American way.

They must not be made to feel that they are mere automatons, fighting machines, as the men in the armed forces of the dictators have been made to feel.

Life in our navy and army is hard. Discipline is tough. It must be. But there also

must be moments when the sailor or soldier is treated as Mr. Somebody-or-other.

That's where the USO comes in. For the USO is the banding together of six great agencies to serve one great purpose—to see that our boys in the camps and naval stations have a place to go, to turn to, a "home away from home."

The duties of the USO have more than doubled during the past year. Its field of operations has been enlarged to include almost the entire face of the globe.

To carry on its all-important work, it needs funds. It needs your contribution. No matter how small you make that contribution, it needs it. *Now.*

You are beset by requests for help on all sides. By all means, try to meet those requests. But among them, be sure not to neglect the USO.

Send your contribution to your local USO committee, or to USO, National Headquarters, Empire State Building, New York.

Give to the USO

Some ads made military life seem almost jolly. By its very nature, advertising highlighted the positive and heroic sides of the experience. Some ads, however, showed the unvarnished downside, such as this June 1942 plea from the USO. The USO received funding from the National War Fund and was a federation of six agencies (the YMCA, YWCA, National Catholic Community Service, National Jewish Welfare Board, Salvation Army, and National Travelers Aid Association), plus the affiliated USO-Camp Shows. The artist who drew the illustration in this ad was Albert Dorne, who produced several war posters for other agencies, including the Army Conservation Program and the OWI.

The comics had their opponents, as well. "One of our bitterest, most long-drawn-out arguments with the Army was over the allocation of newsprint to newspapers, especially for Sunday editions," wrote Donald Nelson in *Arsenal of Democracy*. "Time and again I heard Judge Patterson argue that the production of comic strips and Sunday 'funny papers' entailed a waste of critical material which could be stopped, and on innumerable occasions I was sharply attacked by the Army for permitting the use of newsprint for this purpose. But I fought back. . . ." Nelson took this to mean that the army thought the government should tell publishers what they could publish, a step much too close to censorship, he thought.

The concept of "truth" in wartime media quickly becomes tangled up in the problems of censorship, propaganda, and morale. Censorship is a well-recognized fact of wartime communications, and it played a heavy role during both world wars. On April 13, 1917, a week after the United States had declared war on Germany, President Wilson created the Committee on Public Information (headed by George Creel). The secretaries of state, war, and the navy were members. It "did much more than set up a voluntary program of restricting publication of military secrets," wrote Byron Price, who was director of censorship during World War II. "It set about mobilizing public opinion behind the war effort by providing a mass of news stories, articles, pictures, posters, speeches, and other patriotic material. It handled government publicity, including many of the functions of the OWI during the second war."

The role of the Office of Censorship, created December 16, 1941, was much more narrowly defined, although the agency's staff grew to 15,000. Price promised that the Office of Censorship would make "no attempt . . . to prevent the people from learning the progress of the war from day to day or to curtail their expression of opinion on the conduct of the war." In 1942, however, he cautioned, "Broadcasters were requested to exercise extraordinary care over all programs in which the public has easy access to the microphone. In an impromptu 'man in the street' program of interviews, for instance, an enemy agent might utter a seemingly innocent sentence which would contain an important secret signal."

As a result, weather forecasts for extended areas were restricted on the grounds that they might help enemy ships or planes plan attack routes. Oldsmobile started a "Buy a Bomber" campaign in May 1943, and

Next page
Showing a graveyard would have been unheard of at the beginning of the war, when Americans were still officially shielded from the carnage of combat. In those early, naive days, a phrase such as "We fell under their guns like wheat to the blade of the reaper" would have been horrifying; even today, it is still moving. This ad appeared in February 1944. Courtesy, White Consolidated Industries, Inc.

"FOR JOE AND PETE AND JACK AND HARRY..."

We took the beach-head at dawn.

Our destroyers stood out to sea and threw in the shells and our planes pounded hell out of their pill boxes, and then we came in . . .

But, the wind and the tide tricked us.

The landing boats grounded off shore and we jumped over the sides and stood in the warm, shallow water and stared at the far-away beach and then at each other . . . and our eyes and our mouths were wide with fear as we waded in . . .

And we fell under their guns like wheat to the blade of the reaper. And though they said we could never take it . . . at dawn on the third day we took it.

I'm not fighting for myself alone . . .

I'm fighting for the buddies who fell beside me . . . for Joe and Pete and Jack and Harry. For the flag they loved, and their kids back home, and the faith they held in their right to be free . . . for the future and the life that they gave up . . . for the things that make America the one country in all the world where a man can be somebody . . . where a man can go somewhere.

I know why I'm still out here.

I know what's got to be done.

And I'm not coming back until I'm through with my knife and my gun . . . until I know that terrorism and the lust to kill and enslave are forever dead . . . until all men and women and children can live without fear . . . as free *individuals* in a land, and a world, where there will always be liberty, equality and freedom of opportunity.

That's what they fought and died for.

That's what I'm fighting for.

That's America.

Keep it that way until I come back.

. . .

Here at Nash-Kelvinator we're building Pratt & Whitney engines for the Navy's Vought Corsairs and Grumman Hellcats . . . Hamilton Standard propellers for United Nations bombers . . . governors, binoculars, parts for ships, jeeps, tanks and trucks . . . readying production lines for Sikorsky helicopters. All of us devoted to winning this war . . . to speeding the Peace when our men will come back to their jobs and homes and even better futures than they had before . . . to the day when together we'll build an even finer Kelvinator, an even greater Nash!

The Army-Navy "E" awarded to Nash-Kelvinator Corp., Propeller Division

NASH-KELVINATOR CORPORATION
Kenosha · Milwaukee · DETROIT · Grand Rapids · Lansing

LET'S ALL BACK THE ATTACK!
BUY EXTRA WAR BONDS.

NASH
AUTOMOBILES
KELVINATOR
REFRIGERATORS · ELECTRIC RANGES

"I WILL COME HOME AGAIN..."

Out here, I hope...;

Out here, I think...

Out here, I dream of peace—and coming home to showers and clean sheets and Christmas trees and apple pies and my job... and the girl I love.

I *will* come home again...

But not until my brother's eyes no longer watch a red sun rising on Bataan. Not until men I've marched and eaten with no longer sleep beside forgotten beaches. Not while men who suffered, bled and died for me are unavenged.

No...

Not yet, before we strike down the enemy ... and gut his ships and strip his guns, and break his will to hate and lust and kill.

No terms...

No paper peace put down by foes who,

lacking guns, will still fight with pen and ink—can rob me of the victory I've bought with heart's blood and sweat and grief.

I'll come home again when this war's won...

I'll turn to the job I want to do, when I'm done with this job that *must* be done... and not before. I'll come home again, when I'm free from the hate and greed of other men ... when I'm free of war and the restraints of war ... when I'll be free to plan a future of my own ... free to build an even better America—an even better world—than the one I've always known. Free to work and be honored for my work in a land where there will always be for me and every man liberty, security and dignity ... and the opportunity to set my pace and win my place according to my own ability.

That's what this war's about.

That's what Victory will be for.

That's what I want when I come home.

* * *

Night and day we're driving on to Victory ... building 2,000 h.p. Pratt & Whitney engines for Navy Vought Corsair fighting planes ... making intricate Hamilton Standard propellers for United Nations bombers ... readying production lines to build Sikorsky helicopters for the Army Air Forces ... producing other important items of ordnance ...

For we believe there can be no peace without Victory ... but we believe we can and must win this war soon ... help bring our sons and brothers back again to their jobs and homes and even better futures than they had before. And, together, turn to peaceful things — to the building of an even finer Kelvinator, an even greater Nash.

* * *

NASH-KELVINATOR CORPORATION

Kenosha • Milwaukee • DETROIT • Grand Rapids • Lansing

NASH
AUTOMOBILES
KELVINATOR
REFRIGERATORS • ELECTRIC RANGES

Let's Get It Over With Quick!
Buy More War Bonds Now!

134

Enemy Propaganda. The salient question was whether we should have been directing propaganda at ourselves.

Bruce Barton had been an isolationist before the war and worked in the advertising industry during it. In Stephen Fox's book *The Mirror Makers,* Barton answered this question when he described advertising's contributions to the war effort: "We did not tell the truth, of course. We simply set forth in pictures and copy the Administration's war argument. . . . This was sound and patriotic and moral while the war lasted."

Some observers and historians thought that wartime coverage was extremely effective. According to Lester Markel, it "was not done by preaching or by exhortation or by piling on of color and of adjectives, but by the simple, swift, true narration of events." Cameras didn't lie, and news photographers were dodging bullets and clicking away on all combat fronts.

If some of the news coverage and some of the advertising pictures were somewhat deceptive, according to Paul Fussell, it was due to "the normal human talent for looking on the bright side, for not receiving information likely to cause distress or occasion a major overhaul of normal ethical, political or psychological assumptions." The "whole" story rarely made it into contemporary accounts and, to some extent, never made it into many history books that were written later. "I don't mean that the correspondents were liars," John Steinbeck said in 1977. "It is in the things not mentioned that the untruth lies."

The Allies won, of course, and that fact excuses much of the excess and overreaction of those who dealt with information during the war.

Roy Porter, a writer for Wide World Features during the war, once wrote a story that explained the war's progress, and historian Lee Kennett later described Porter's account: "He could give very few hard figures—the censors had done their work well. But he maintained an exuberant optimism and he used the same sort of superlatives that other writers had used on the 1941 maneuvers and the B-17 bomber: the United States was becoming 'the greatest military colossus in the world.' Yet such phrases were no longer extravagant. As with the news accounts of Midway, what was reported approached reality—or perhaps reality was catching up with reportage."

You Can't Keep a Good Man Down!

JACK KELLY
SEAMAN, TWICE TORPEDOED
IS BACK AT SEA

Twice, Jack Kelly heard the ear-splitting explosion of a torpedo ripping into his ship. Each time his tanker was lost. Each time he was picked up later by a life boat.

But twice wasn't too much for Kelly. Like many another Socony-Vacuum tanker seaman—torpedoed a number of times — Kelly went back for more!

When you picture oil-soaked Jack Kelly being dragged aboard a life boat, your own lot as a

civilian doesn't seem so tough.

One of the reasons motorists don't mind so much doing with less gasoline is the realization of what the tanker crews go through to get oil to them and the armed forces. They are among the unsung heroes of the war.

Unswerving loyalty to their work makes us proud not only of all these Jack Kellys, but also of all the 58,000 Socony-Vacuum people at their wartime jobs.

Their record is sensational in the minimum of work hours lost.

In time of peace our people work to make the company behind the Red Horse Sign U.S.A.'s foremost oil company—and give you better motoring. Today, in time of war, they are giving their utmost in service and in products to our country . . . and to you.

SOCONY-VACUUM OIL CO., INC., and Affiliates: Magnolia Petroleum Co., General Petroleum Corp. of California.

Mobilgas
SOCONY-VACUUM

TUNE IN RAYMOND GRAM SWING — Blue Network
Coast-to-Coast, 10 P.M., E.W.T., Mon. Tues. Wed. Thurs.

In Peace or War—
The Sign of Friendly Service Serves America Well!

136

Chapter 6

The Ads And Reality

"A Legend With The Edges Neatly Trimmed"

When Roland Marchand researched his monumental study of the ads of the 1920s and 1930s, *Advertising the American Dream*, he evaluated 180,000 advertisements. His observations and conclusions help illuminate wartime ads, as well. Some of the specific genres—especially those that seem odd and foreign today—had roots in the advertising of the previous decades.

The form of advertisements appears simple and somewhat repetitive: a picture, a headline, a couple columns of copy. Their initial purpose, of course, was to convince and persuade; they sought to motivate the reader to take some action, usually to buy a product, or to accept some idea or belief. Within that structure, the ads produced a wide variety of effects, and we can understand them on several intellectual levels.

For starters, we can respond to these ads with a good deal of simple enjoyment. The quality of the artwork or photography (such as the ads from Coca-Cola or Milky Way and the combat illustrations in the aircraft and automobile ads) remains striking. In some ads, the cleverness of the writing ensures that they are still effective. Some ads make us nostalgic; we remember or imagine a time when the country was truly united, when good and bad were crisply depicted. Other ads are interesting because they vividly show how much things have changed since the early 1940s.

The relationship between the advertiser and the target audience, Marchand found, was surprisingly complex. The people who read the ads were like people who willingly undergo hypnosis. The hypnotist can make them act like chickens, perhaps, but he can't

make them do anything that they wouldn't do ordinarily. Ads can persuade, but they can't force. And if advertisers sometimes depicted a fantasy world, they were giving the target audience what it wanted and

The carnage of combat, which would appear more and more frequently later in the war, seemed far away from this morale-boosting scene of October 1942. Milky Way ran a series of similar ads that today seem strikingly nostalgic. Courtesy, Mars, Inc.

Previous page
Ads such as this one presented an encouraging picture to the folks at home. That America had such handsome, hearty heroes involved in the war effort—notably, here a civilian sailor—doubtlessly boosted morale. This ad is at the polar extreme from an ad such as "What did you do today, for freedom?", shown in Chapter 6. Reprinted with permission of Mobil Corp.

what it would accept. "People did not usually want ads to reflect themselves, their immediate social relationships, or their broader society exactly," Marchand wrote. "They wanted not a true mirror but a Zerrspiegel, a distorting mirror that would enhance certain images." Consumers wanted useful information, but at the same time, they wanted their wishes fulfilled.

Many of advertising's discoveries about what consumers wanted and would accept in 1920s and 1930s directly relate to the themes and genres of ads in the 1940s. Many of the so-called official ads of World War II encouraged readers and told them how to do their bit; earlier advertisers had "discovered a market for broader counsel and reassurance. . . . offering expertise and solace in the face of those modern complexities," Marchand wrote.

Many of the ads that discuss rationing and conservation find counterparts in ads of the 1920s and 1930s that (in contrast to the much less sophisticated ads of the turn of the century) concentrated on the consumer, rather than the product. This approach was custom-

Have a "Coke" = Good winds have blown you here

. . . a way to say "We are friends" to the Chinese

In far-off places, when Coca-Cola is on hand, you find it cementing friendships for our fighting men. China knew Coca-Cola from Tientsin to Shanghai, from Hong Kong to Tsingtao. To Chinese and Yank alike, *Have a "Coke"* are welcome words. They belong with friendliness and freedom. From Atlanta to the Seven Seas, Coca-Cola stands for

the pause that refreshes—has become a symbol of good will among the friendly-minded.

*   *   *

Our fighting men are delighted to meet up with Coca-Cola many places overseas. Coca-Cola has been a globe-trotter "since way back when". Even with war, Coca-Cola today is being bottled right on the spot in over 35 allied and neutral nations.

"Coke" = Coca-Cola
It's natural for popular names to inspire friendly abbreviations. That's why you hear Coca-Cola called "Coke".

Coca-Cola
·the global high-sign·

COPYRIGHT 1943, THE COCA-COLA COMPANY

According to the slogan at lower right, Coca-Cola is "the global high-sign." Coke's European manager recalled, "In 1943 a [German] prisoner-of-war coming down a gangplank at an American port, spotted a bright red sign. He stopped in amazement. 'Oh,' he said to a guard, 'You have Coca-Cola here too!'" Courtesy, The Coca-Cola Co.

made for the wartime situation when manufacturers no longer had commercial products on the market. These consumer-directed ads offered what Marchand called "detailed vignettes of social life," in which the reader "lives" through imaginary experiences in which a product (or its absence) played a part.

Even though the initial and predominant use of print advertising was to sell specific products, there were precedents for the non-product-oriented ads of the war years. A notable example, in 1908, was the series of AT&T ads that set forth the case for a "regulated private monopoly" in the telephone industry.

During World War I, the National War Advisory Board also paved the way for a recurrent element in the ads of the Second World War, because (according to Marchand) they "convinced the nation that advertising could instill new ideas and inspire people to patriotic action." A similar phenomenon took place in England, proving that "advertising was no mere commercial tool, but a great moral and educative force, capable of serving 'unselfish social purposes.'"

Clearly, advertising could do much more than convince a consumer to buy a certain brand of toothpaste. The various tones (seductive, reverent, teasing, scolding) and techniques mustered by the creator of an ad lent themselves to a variety of other purposes.

For example, the "guilt ads" genre of World War II ads descended from a trend that appeared in the 1920s known as "scare copy," also known in ad jargon as "negative appeal." Its goal was to change the consumer's behavior by dramatizing social failures and the critical judgments of fellow citizens. This technique lent itself effectively to treatments of black market cheats, conservation scofflaws, and other homefront slackers.

Some of the more experienced members of the advertising profession may have gotten some practice in writing the morale-boosting ads of World War II during the Depression, when, as Marchand pointed out, they "found ample reason to favor inspirational messages." From 1929 to 1930, ad lineage and revenue declined more than 12 percent, with even steeper declines during the next three years, "creating an eager market for morale-boosting pronouncements."

In any case, by the time the War Advertising Council (WAC) launched its campaigns of World War II, there were a number of potent precedents and expe-

Next page
The Coca-Cola Company developed an ice-making machine and beverage dispenser called a "Jungle Unit" that could be carried on a vehicle as small as a jeep. "By the end of 1944, these units were to be found all over the South Pacific," a company history said. Courtesy, The Coca-Cola Co.

Page 140
Reprinted with permission of Texaco, Inc.

138

Have a "Coke" = Pukka Gen
(SWELL INFO.)

...or how friends are made in the R. A. F.

Have a "Coke" is a friendly greeting among R.A.F. flyers back at early dawn from a night mission. It's a salute among comrades in arms that seals the bonds of friendship in Plymouth, England, as in Plymouth, Mass. It's an offer as welcome on an English airfield as it is in your own living room. Around the globe, Coca-Cola stands for *the pause that refreshes*,—has become a happy symbol of good-hearted friendliness.

*   *   *

Our fighting men are delighted to meet up with Coca-Cola many places overseas. Coca-Cola has been a globe-trotter "since way back when". Even with war, Coca-Cola today is being bottled right on the spot in over 35 allied and neutral nations.

Coca-Cola
-the global high-sign

"Coke" = Coca-Cola
It's natural for popular names to acquire friendly abbreviations. That's why you hear Coca-Cola called "Coke".

...wonder what a "goose-stepper" thinks about?

"Left...right...don't think...left... right...don't think. The Fuehrer thinks for us. Victory soon. Americans soft. Their tanks no good, planes no good. The Fuehrer says so. Left...right...don't think."

* * *

No, Hans, don't think, or you'll falter. Don't think of the American soldiers arriving in Europe, don't think of the great armada of planes and tanks and guns rolling off America's production lines behind them.

Don't think of the vast American oil fields which feed the tanks and guns and planes . . . oil for which your Fuehrer would give many, many thousands of

"superior Aryan" lives like yours.

The Texas Company alone produces far more oil than all of Europe . . . oil for 100-octane aviation gasoline . . . oil for Toluene to make TNT, oil for Butadiene, basis of synthetic rubber. We are just one company. Hundreds more are working on other parts of our vast fighting machine.

No . . . don't think, Hans. But soon you will feel . . . and unfortunately your Fuehrer cannot feel for you.

THE TEXAS COMPANY

TEXACO FIRE-CHIEF AND SKY-CHIEF GASOLINES
GASOLINE AND TEXACO MOTOR OILS

140

riences on which ad writers could draw. The WAC's influence is clearly illustrated in many of the advertisements shown in this book. That is not to say that the WAC approved or guided all of the advertising of the war years, or that all of it was successful or admirable. Some ads seemed popular, but others generated criticism.

The WAC tried to anticipate potential controversies in its definition of war advertising by excluding three genres of ads. First, it excluded what would become known as "brag advertising," in which companies or trade groups boasted about their own achievements. Second, it ruled out "political" advertising aimed at extolling private enterprise and capitalism. Third, the WAC tried to discourage advertising that fantasized about the wonderful postwar world. All three of these excluded genres are amply represented in this book's selection, and sometimes the distinctions blur.

The phenomenon of brag advertising is an intriguing aspect of wartime ads and a topic that stirred up considerable sound and fury both during the war and in the critical analysis since. The problem wasn't minor and was officially recognized at the highest levels. To the Commerce Department's way of thinking, it was perfectly acceptable for an advertiser to call the public's attention to some aspect of the war effort and to explain its company's contribution to that effort. Proponents of this approach thought that the ads helped build morale early in the war by instilling confidence.

In *Advertising and Its Role in War and Peace*, a Commerce Department official wrote, "Some of the more unfortunate examples seemed to imply that the manufacturers of relatively unimportant items were winning the war all by themselves." Or, as one commentator put it, they claimed "mountainous importance for molehills of achievement." Raymond Rubicam quoted a serviceman in his essay in the book *While You Were Gone:* " 'When I read the ads I don't see why I'm here in camp. We don't need men in this war—our machines are so perfect they'll do the job themselves.' "

According to a written summary of the OWI and Graphic Arts Victory Committee Conference on March 26, 1943, H. Gardner Cowles, Jr. (director of Domestic Operations for the OWI) "called attention to the increase in 'pat-on-the-back' advertising, now being used by many companies with no goods to sell but desirous of keeping their names before the public. The feeling has been growing in Washington, Cowles said, that advertising of this nature should be prohibited, since it uses critical materials and manpower and does not help in the conduct of the war. Pointing out that curtailment could be achieved by a ruling of the Bureau of Internal Revenue disallowing the expense, he suggested that advertising can forestall such a limitation by getting behind the war and helping to solve problems on the homefront."

Other ads erred by trying to be clever or cute. One manufacturer of cast-iron pipes created an ad that showed a soldier telling his girlfriend not to worry

Although much of the advertising of the war was "something new under the sun," in the words of a contemporary writer, some of the morale-boosting pep talks found precedent in ads of the Depression, which were not commercial and didn't involve products. This ad appeared in December 1933, as part of the Mobilization for Human Needs campaign.

Next page
Reprinted with permission of Texaco, Inc.

Page 143
In this ad, Armstrong obliquely deals with a controversial topic: "brag advertising," presenting it in a disarming way. The Armstrong Company had had experience during World War I, when it produced shells and camouflage materials. It set up a Munitions Division in 1941; during the next five years, it would produce 22 million army shells of seven types. Company employees became involved in the war effort in numerous ways. At the two Lancaster plants in 1943, workers submitted 4,170 suggestions for improving methods and safety. At Pittsburgh, pigeon fanciers began raising their birds to meet the requirements for army carrier pigeons. Courtesy, Armstrong World Industries, Inc.

"What do you mean ...
EX-service man ?"

The sergeant grinned as he slipped me
my mustering out orders:

*"Well, where do you go from here, EX-
service man?"*

"Kindly omit the 'EX,'" I said. *"I was a service man long before I got into this man's army,
a Texaco Service man, and I'll be one again
when I get home."*

As a Texaco Dealer, I'll have something the
motorist can't get anywhere else — a swell line-
up of special service features. My business will
grow, just as it did before the war, because
people *like* Texaco's Registered Rest Rooms,
Circle Service and all the others.

*"Drive into my station some time, Sarge, and
see what a real service man can do for your car!"*

THE TEXAS COMPANY

A great postwar line-up

You're welcome at
TEXACO DEALERS
TUNE IN . . . Texaco Star Theatre every Sunday night starring
James Melton. Complete Metropolitan Opera broadcasts every
Saturday afternoon. See newspapers for time and stations.

142

"Don't try to tell us your old company is winning the war!"

TOM: I didn't say that. Didn't even mention the war stuff we're making. All I said was that Armstrong Cork is tied up—one way or another—with almost everything we're using—or wearing—or eating.

CHIEF: Eating? Oh, you mean that Armstrong's Linoleum you're so proud of down there in the galley.

TOM: Sure, but that's just one angle. Look—there's Armstrong's Insulation in our refrigerator, a lot of our chow comes in glass jars that we make, and . . .

S. P.: And I suppose these shoes of mine have got linoleum soles?

TOM: No, but I betcha there's plenty of our stuff in 'em—bottom filler and box toes, for instance—and, take your uniform . . .

S. P.: What about my uniform?

TOM: Betcha the yarn in the cloth was made on a textile machine that had our cork roll coverings on it.

S. P.: The kid can sure hand it out, eh?

CHIEF: Yah! Let's see how good he is at handing out those cigarettes he's hiding—and don't try to tell us Armstrong is in the tobacco business, too.

TOM: Got you there, Chief! Take a look at the cork tips on these cigarettes. We make 'em by the millions.

S. P.: Well, what do you know? Darned if that old outfit of yours doesn't make a lot of different things.

YES, WE MAKE MANY THINGS—more than 360 of them, in fact—and Tom is pretty nearly right when he says that Armstrong products have something to do, directly or indirectly, with almost everything you can think of.

Just to give you an idea—insulating fire brick helps make metal products—cork covering on refrigerated lines helps refine petroleum—gaskets and oil seals go into all kinds of machinery—glass insulators play an important part in communication—and so on through the long list of industries that use products made by the Company you know best as the maker of Armstrong's Linoleum, Asphalt Tile, and Quaker Rugs.

Now we are busy making many new products—fuselage sections and parts for fighting planes, shot, shells, cartridge cases, incendiary bombs, camouflage netting, and dozens of other things that give us a place with the thousands of American companies whose first interest today is helping to win the war.

ARMSTRONG
CORK COMPANY

Makers of hundreds of products for Home, Industry, and Victory

Lancaster, Pa.; Camden, N. J.; Pittsburgh, Pa.; Millville, N. J.; Beaver Falls, Pa.; Fulton, N. Y.; Dunkirk, Ind.; Philadelphia, Pa.; So. Braintree, Mass.; Gloucester, N. J.; Pensacola, Fla.; Keyport, N. J.; South Gate, Cal.

143

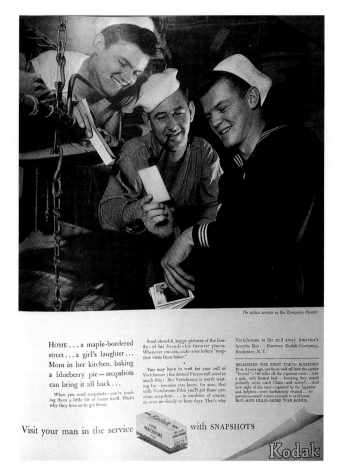

On active service in the European theater.

HOME . . . a maple-bordered street . . . a girl's laughter . . . Mom in her kitchen, baking a blueberry pie — snapshots can bring it all back . . .

When you send snapshots — you're sending them a little bit of home itself. That's why they love so to get them.

Send cheerful, happy pictures of the family — of his friends — his favorite places. Whenever you can, make your letters' snapshot visits from home."

You may have to wait for your roll of Verichrome (the Armed Forces still need so much film). But Verichrome is worth waiting for — because you know, for sure, that with Verichrome Film you'll get those precious snapshots . . . in sunshine, of course, or even on cloudy or hazy days. That's why

Verichrome is far and away America's favorite film . . . Eastman Kodak Company, Rochester, N. Y.

REMEMBER THE FIRST TOKYO BOMBING? How, 3 years ago, our flyers took off from the carrier "Hornet" — 740 miles off the Japanese coast . . . into a gale, with limited fuel . . . knowing they would probably never reach China — and what then? . . . And how eight of the men — captured by the Japanese and helpless — were barbarously treated . . . reported executed? A stern example to us at home. BUY-AND HOLD-MORE WAR BONDS.

Visit your man in the service with SNAPSHOTS

Kodak

Kodak's roots reach back to the Eastman Dry Plate Company in 1881; the name "Kodak" was trademarked in 1888. During World War I, the company developed aerial cameras and trained aerial photographers for the US Army Signal Corps. It supplied cellulose acetate for the wings of navy aircraft, and produced unbreakable lenses for gas masks. In 1941, the company developed the "Airgraph" (or V-Mail) system for microfilming letters to conserve shipping space. This ad balances a warm, comfortable view of sailors with a mini-documentary about Doolittle's Tokyo Raid. The ad appeared in May 1945. Reprinted courtesy of Eastman Kodak Co.

because he was as tough as the cast-iron pipe. The anthropomorphic notion that inanimate objects somehow "went to war" seemed to annoy lots of soldiers. One serviceman was quoted as complaining, "As soon as a pea canner runs short of peas he shouts, 'Canned peas have gone to war!'" One account of the war years tells the story of a veteran copywriter who had been wounded twice and had been discharged from the army. On his return stateside, he warned advertisers that G.I.s overseas were disgusted by American advertising in which companies were boasting that their products were helping win the war, when in fact victory was still on the far horizon.

A typical "here's what we're doing" ad was published by Brown Shoe Company (makers of a brand

Which comes first —
Your second helping?
or our second front?

You want to see this war won — and won quickly. You want to see it carried to the enemy with a vengeance. Okay — so do all of us. But just remember . . .

A second front takes food . . . food to feed our allies *in addition* to our own men.

Which do you want — more meat for you, or enough meat for them? An extra cup of coffee on your breakfast table, or a full tin cup of coffee for a fighting soldier?

Just remember that the meat you don't get — and the coffee and the sugar that you don't get — are up at the front lines — fighting for you.

Would you have it otherwise?

CHEERFULLY CO-OPERATING with rationing is one way we can help to win this war. But there are scores of others. Many of them are described in a new free booklet called "You and the War," available from this magazine. Send for your copy today! Learn about the many opportunities for doing an important service to your country. Read about the Citizens Defense Corps, organized as part of Local Defense Councils. Choose the job you're best at, and start doing it! You're needed — now!

EVERY CIVILIAN A FIGHTER

The "Every Civilian a Fighter" series of public-service ads was an effective contribution of the Magazine Publishers of America. This installment, from June 1943, bluntly put rationing in perspective.

called Roblee) in May 1943. A picture of three civilian dress shoes for men dominates the ad, but the lower third is a sidebar that shows a combat boot, a soldier running and carrying a rifle with bayonet attached, and the following text beneath a headline that says "The Fightin'est Shoes in the World . . .":

The mothers and fathers of all the Bills and Franks and Jims who are in this fight will be interested to know that their sons are not only the best fed but the most comfortably clothed and the best shod fighting men in the world.

During World War I it was often said that shoes came in only two sizes — "too big and too small." Today our Army is equipped with shoes in *all* sizes from 5 to 15 and in widths all the way from A to EE. They are made of the finest leathers, over the best fitting lasts ever developed.

What's more, we are building shoes for the various battle conditions our men and allies are meeting — Russian Combat boots, Paratrooper boots, Combination rubber-leather Yukon Pacs, as well as the regulation Navy and Army Service Shoes.

Brown Shoe Company salutes these men in service and dedicates to them its vast resources and 65 years of shoemaking experience. We are proud to be one of the manufacturers selected to make "battle brogans" for fighting forces.

It was the means, not the end, that caused problems. In the case of brag ads, the problems were far from minor. "As the war continued such advertisements were pilloried not only by servicemen, civilians, and government officials, but increasingly by advertising men as well," Raymond Rubicam wrote in *While You Were Gone.*

In his book *The Diary of an Ad Man,* James Webb Young recorded his thoughts midway through the war. "The boys who are helping the Advertising Council prepare campaigns for government purposes are making a mistake," he wrote. "They are using too many of the conventional tricks of the trade in their copy. The public is in no mood for this when it comes to war aims. All they want and need is to be told simply, clearly and authoritatively what they should do."

Print ads weren't the only culprits. On the subject of radio, Norman Corwin wrote of several instances of poor taste that were broadcast after Pearl Harbor. For example, "Here is a late important news bulletin: Use Smith Brothers Cough Drops." Another ad recommended a brand of razor blade because it lasted longer, thereby "conserving steel" for national defense. According to Corwin, the radio industry adopted restrictions on commercials that tried to "capitalize" on the war. For example, a series of cigarette ads was banned because they used the sounds of gunfire, airplane motors, and ship's horns, sound effects that were too close to the real thing.

In *Days of Sadness, Years of Triumph,* Geoffrey Perrett added another example: "Not a little of the advertising was blatantly offensive, especially when juxtaposed with incoming war news," he wrote. "New Yorkers were startled one night to hear reports of heavy American casualties followed by a funeral home commercial: 'You never know when to expect bad news. So be prepared. Buy a family plot.'"

In his essay in *While You Were Gone,* Paul Gallico discussed "the first open revolt against the nauseating institutional advertising flooding the magazines and air waves." According to Gallico, the producer of the pop-

---

"Home of the Brave"

Pure sentiment and hometown idealism reach a pinnacle in this June 1943 advertisement from Goodyear Aircraft. Borrowing the final line of the "Star Spangled Banner," the ad is among the earliest to deal with the deaths of military personnel. The blue star on a service flag meant that the soldier it symbolized was alive; a gold star meant that he or she had been killed. The flags were an emotion-laden and common symbol on wartime ads.

It's a simple home, one of uncounted thousands very much alike.

An unpretentious place, with a bit of well-tended garden in the summer, and yellow light streaming ready welcome from its windows at night.

It's a home that once rang with the noise and tumult a healthy boy can make, a home pleasant with fragrant kitchen smells and comfortable with the worn hollows of familiar and friendly furniture.

It's a home where hope has been born, where suffering has been met, where great plans have been laid and achievements, big and little, have been celebrated.

Now, suddenly, over it a shadow falls.

The time has come when the brave flag with the star of blue on it must come down, so that one with a star of gold may take its place.

This is war, and war is striking home.

Striking at the simple, the peace-loving homes where live those who must now be the bravest of the brave.

What can you say to those whose hearts bear the aching burden of this conflict?

That their sons have died in a noble cause?

That the nation mourns with them in their bereavement?

That these men shall be avenged, that we shall see to it that they shall not have died in vain?

No, you can't say these things and have them really mean anything.

You can't say anything—you can only do.

You can only bend a bit more grimly to whatever task is yours in these stern times.

You can only try, a little harder than you thought you could, to make sure that no boy, yours or any other's, falls because of anything you do or leave undone.

You can only pull tight your belt, and buy to the limit of your ability the War Bonds it takes to equip our fighting men.

You can only fall in line with friend and neighbor and, through scrap drives and conservation campaigns, play your part as fully as you can, as every good soldier on the home front should.

You can only remember that every helpful act, no matter how small, not only hastens Victory but does its share to bring more boys back before their blue stars turn to gold.

Here at Goodyear we have a service flag of our own.

Already it is beginning to show a tinge of gold.

Because it is, everything we build—every airship, every plane, every life raft, every barrage balloon, tire, wheel, brake, bullet-puncture-sealing fuel tank and fuel line—is built with something more than just the thought of building *all* we can as fast as we can.

It is built also with the idea of doing the *best* we can—that fewer gold stars shall hang in the simple homes of the brave.

ular program 'Information Please' took away sponsorship from Lucky Strike because the producer "couldn't stomach Lucky's line—'Lucky Strike Green has gone to war,' referring to the color on the package. Heinz got the show, which went merrily on."

Brag ads became such a well-recognized and controversial genre that a few ads made fun of the approach. Raymond Rubicam cited a lipstick ad that said, "It won't build morale, it won't preserve our way of life, all [this] lipstick will do is make you look prettier. If it's victory you want, better buy bonds."

It should be pointed out that advertisers had serious problems to solve during the war. They had to explain why some products were missing or available only in limited quantities. And, in Rubicam's words, they faced the risk that "what was offensive in peace was ten times more so in war." Many ads were not offensive, many drew mixed reviews, and still others were quite effective. Nevertheless, Rubicam wrote, "If 'fertilizer can win the war' as still another advertiser claimed, the brag ads were surely spreading it around" early in the war.

"Guilt ads" were another recognizable sub-group. In retrospect, some seem grossly exaggerated. One ad tried to convince people to avoid buying black market goods: "Did you drown a sailor today because YOU bought a lamb chop without giving up the required coupons?" The connection is hard to follow.

A classic guilt ad came from the Gruen Watch Company; it shows a jaunty, pipe-smoking soldier walking with a cane. "Tell Steve you cashed your War Bond," it says. "He got his new legs yesterday. This morning, just about the time you were cashing that War Bond, he was trying them out on the hospital porch. His steps weren't as brisk as yours. . . . You want others to win *your* war. Steve would like his own legs back. But he's not asking for his money back. *Soldiers* aren't cashing their War Bonds."

Some ads were plain and blunt. Others cajoled or teased the reader. Still others scolded; one showed a civilian lounging on his living-room couch. "Just sleep right through the war," the ad copy said. "Let some other guy do your share! What's it to you that a kid just got bumped off in the Solomons . . . because you couldn't be bothered with scrap collection? Sure, you outsmarted the ration board on gas all right . . . and kept

Mothers of soldiers were frequent characters in ads, usually in sentimental circumstances, although this March 1943 ad is on the cornier end of the spectrum. Courtesy, American Gas Assoc.

a certain Army plane in Africa out of the air . . . Come on, get off that fat can of yours . . . stop riding and start pushing!"

Another far-from-subtle ad showed three young girls lined up along a wall in a Nazi headquarters with a Nazi official leering at them. "A high honor for your daughter," the text said, mentioning that "she may be a perfect specimen for one of their experimental camps." Another showed a hangman's noose, with a smaller picture in the background of five people hanging. "Try this for size. This type of collar is designed for conquered people. . . ."

While debate raged on the homefront over whether advertising was necessary and whether it should be permitted, anecdotal evidence trickled in from the front lines. At various times during the war, to save space or conserve paper, a few special editions of publications were distributed overseas minus the usual

147

BACK HOME FOR KEEPS

He's the man of your heart. He's the light of your life. He's all you want to live for . . . live *with*. And some day (fling out a rainbow!), some glad morning, he'll be home. You'll hear his step on the stair. You'll move into the tight circle of his arms . . . *forever*.

Some day! Yes, it's for *that* day we of Community* are living, too. Thinking about it, while we work at our war jobs. Planning for it—planning brightly gleaming silverware for brides who never had a home, patterns as enduring as your postwar world together. Our craftsmen's hands keep their skill. Our designers' hearts hold fast their dream. We know—with you—*the day will come!*

BUY WAR BONDS! SPEED THE DAY!

Community
THE FINEST SILVERPLATE

"Lady Hamilton Design

If its Community . . . its correct

This classic end-of-the-war ad from May 1945 belies the massive production of the Ford Motor Company. Ford totals included 278,000 jeeps, 93,000 military trucks, 27,000 tank engines, nearly 14,000 universal carriers, 12,500 armored cars, 87,000 aircraft generators, and 53,000 superchargers. Courtesy, Ford Motor Co.

This fascinating ad from Cannon (January 1944) ranks high on the list of cheerful and amusing views of the war. Before the war, Fieldcrest-Cannon mainly produced "huck" towels, a flat weave of cotton familiar in hotels, barber shops, and Pullman cars. During the war, "most of our towel production went overseas," explained company historian and editor Jim Monroe. The company substituted the terry-loop towel for use on the homefront, and it proved so popular that it took over the market after the war. The company celebrated its centennial in 1987. In the fine print at the upper right is the name of the advertising company that designed this ad: N.W. Ayer & Son. The June 28, 1943, issue of Ayer's company newsletter described the research behind Cannon's "How do servicemen bathe?" campaign. "We collected a mountain of 'authorizations'—explained out antecedents innumerable times—signed and countersigned miles of records to secure the material for these advertisements," the newsletter editor reported. "We talked with about 70 officers and scores of enlisted men . . . visited Navy camps, Navy yards, forts—a total of 17 military establishments." Ayer claimed that all the ads were authentic, some documented with photos. "Surveys indicate that this campaign has the appeal to get high readership today: a war slant, pleasurable news of service men, an understanding of the housewife's problems." Courtesy, Fieldcrest Cannon, Inc.

always—built around you and me . . . the kind of 'when we're a family' dreaming we did before you became a Navy flier."

These after-it's-over fantasies (what one writer called "a rash of utopian word-pictures of the postwar product-world") threatened to get out of control toward the end of the war. The WAC promptly issued warnings that the war was not yet finished.

Love wasn't the only emotion to which wartime ads appealed. Some ads spurred anger toward the enemy; others aimed for sorrow. Foremost among the tear-jerkers was a Goodyear ad that showed a mother holding the telegram that had just informed her that her son had been killed in combat.

Critics often complain that ads aren't true to life, that they are unrealistic or deceptive. These critics are sometimes on target, but they ignore the goal of advertising, which isn't the same as that of a maker of documentary films or an investigative journalist. To Roland Marchand, advertising isn't a place to look for the social realities of life, but rather "the semblances and fantasies of that life." After his exhaustive study, Marchand ended up accepting the definition of advertisements as "the clearest indicators of a society's unfulfilled needs,"

and a mechanism that "would buffer their adaptation to modern reality."

The realities of World War II—casualties in the hundreds of thousands, widespread social disruption, and international fear and hatred—certainly required that buffering.

He saw the grave of a nation's freedom

The Corporal never fully realized *what* he was fighting until that April morning in 1945 at Nordhausen, when he found himself beside the long, open grave. There were bodies in it—the bodies of slave-laborers—stripped now of their last defenses, their last dignity.

Strangely enough, his strongest feeling was not one of horror but of sadness. Back in his own free and happy country he'd never dreamed that evil like this could exist anywhere.

The spring breeze stirred the new leaves gently, the sun was bright, but there seemed to be a cold shadow in the sunshine. For the Corporal knew he was looking at the grave of a people's freedom. And he knew that free men could never relax their vigilance against such forces of oppression, whatever label they might bear.

The Corporal—now a Sergeant—still remembers. And he's typical of thousands of Veterans who are rejoining the Army Combat Forces and urging others to join. Alert, intelligent, hard as nails physically—with the best training and equipment and the most powerful weapons in history—they make up a team that can strike with the force of a thunderbolt. These men are proud in the realization that they have one of the most important jobs on earth—keeping our nation strong and free.

Yes, it's a big job, but *real men* are meeting the challenge. Are you man enough to measure up—and take your place beside them? Ask today at your nearest Recruiting Station.

U. S. ARMY AND U. S. AIR FORCE RECRUITING SERVICE

YOUR ARMY AND YOUR AIR FORCE SERVE THE NATION AND MANKIND IN WAR AND PEACE

Chapter 7

How An Ad Agency Entered The Fray

"What's It To You That A Kid Just Got Bumped Off In The Solomons?"

The boom in wartime advertising turned ad agencies into more-than-usually frantic places during the war. They had intimate connections with a spectrum of businesses that were directly affected by the war; as a result, they felt the tremors of global combat well before Pearl Harbor. The large New York firm of N.W. Ayer & Son was typical. The progress of the war can be clearly traced via its newsletter, *Ayer News Files*.

In July 1940, Ayer signed on American Export Lines, Incorporated, as a client, describing the company as "one of the most important arms of the U.S. Merchant Marine." In October, the newsletter reported that the company had transferred a ship to the navy "for defense purposes." An ensuing advertisement "emphasized the value of the American Merchant Marine—in times of peace and in times of threatened danger." German U-boat patrols would soon make that danger more than just a threat.

The US army was another Ayer client. In August 1940, it launched a recruiting campaign to 621 communities aimed at bringing its strength up to its authorized limit of 375,000 by January 1, 1941. In October 1940, the newsletter reported that President Roosevelt had taken the lid off the army's authorized strength, shooting for 500,000, and that Ayer had also been assigned the job of helping recruit 12,500 "Flying Cadets." In July 1941, Ayer announced that the army had reached the goal of 375,000 two-and-a-half months ahead of schedule. The army would later enlist 90,000 volunteers in a single month, January 1942.

Roosevelt's "Arsenal of Democracy" speech triggered an increasing surge of production felt by many of Ayer's clients. In February 1941, American Rolling Mill Company began building a new plant. The Office of Production Management announced that it was "part of plans to expand the steel industry to meet defense needs."

The demands of Lend-Lease aid to the Allies also came into play in Ayer ad strategies. A June 26, 1941, item in the newsletter cited an ad that had been triggered by "various alarms about the possible shortage of gasoline and furnace oil in the East," which in turn "have caused apprehension and uncertainty among the millions who use these products." Ayer reported that the series of ads created for this client was "an excellent example of the way advertising can be used to create good will through understanding, and should go a long way to allay fears which might arise from irresponsible statements about the situation." The ad pointed out that one cause of the shortage was the transfer of fifty American tankers to the British.

As was the case with so many companies during the war, Ayer employees became officially involved with the war effort. Ayer's well-known art director, Charles Coiner, joined with William Phillips of the Office of Emergency Management's (OEM) Information Division and formed a group of two-dozen poster designers to produce posters for government agencies. Coiner's position with the OEM was "technical adviser on design," equivalent to art director. "The work requires him to spend one day a week, plus most week-ends, in

Previous page
N.W. Ayer created this striking ad for the US Army and US Air Force Recruiting Service in 1947. In the years just after the war, most Americans were anxious to forget wartime concerns and get back to normal life, just as many ads during the war kept looking ahead to when it would be over.

Next page
This ad, which marked the anniversary of Pearl Harbor in an unusual way, offered a typically frenetic wartime approach: It plugged a product and a radio show, glanced ahead to "the day of Victory," mentioned savings bonds, and described the company's military contributions in a classically nebulous manner ("the results can be reported in detail only after the war"). The ad was created by N.W. Ayer in late 1943, and appeared in Collier's *on December 11 and* Look *on December 28. Courtesy, The General Electric Hall of History Foundation*

30,000,000 families had washed the dishes that day...

Few Americans will ever forget what they were doing on the Sunday afternoon that fell December 7, 1941.

The sun shone in most parts of the country. A Brahms Concerto welled tranquilly from radios in thousands of peaceful living rooms. And in millions of kitchens, the warm, soapy smell of fresh-washed china and sparkling glassware mingled with the lingering fragrance of Sunday-dinners-done. . . .

In some thousands of homes, Mother and the girls did *NOT* wash the dishes that Sunday. They were consigned to a new contribution to our pre-Pearl Harbor standard of living — a G-E Electric Dishwasher that performs the whole task and leaves them sterilized, shining clean and dry.

Because our men of electrical research and production had made practical this and many other technically complex home conveniences for America, the full force of electricity quickly could be turned against the enemy, arming and protecting our men and sensitizing our fighting machines as the world had never seen it done before. Naturally, every General Electric facility was instantly and whole-heartedly devoted to this effort, with results that can be reported in detail only after the war.

But when the day of Victory dawns, they will return to the peacetime job of making things for better living. Things finer because of General Electric's war experience and research. They will be part of the complete G-E equipment you will take for granted in the new, low-cost home your War Savings Bonds will help to build or buy.

DISHWASHER

EVERYTHING ELECTRICAL FOR AFTER VICTORY HOMES

GENERAL ⬤ ELECTRIC

Washington," the newsletter reported. In *Nine Pioneers in American Graphic Design*, Coiner is quoted as saying, "When I started the government work, people were not conscious of the fact that we were about ready to go into war. We had to get workers steamed up, and a lot of the posters were made for that purpose."

Coiner was no stranger to federal projects. In 1939, he had designed the National Recovery Administration's (NRA) distinctive Blue Eagle. He soon designed the set of insignia used on armbands and helmets of civilian defense volunteers and workers, members of the Citizens' Defense Corps (CDC), later called Civil Defense. Had war broken out on the mainland, the symbols would have helped ambulance drivers, messengers, rescue squads, and auxiliary police. Coiner also designed the symbol for the National War Fund.

During the war, Coiner was art director for a series of Boeing ads. According to the authors of *Nine Pioneers*, "His idea was to make them look like news and information, and not like ads," a technique that was common in wartime ads.

The Ayer newsletter began including a section on what "Ayer and Ayer people are doing in national defense." One item mentioned that an employee was "chairman of the Rockefeller Center Air Raid Defense Class, one of the most important units in the country." Later, in August 1943, an item would report the "First Gold Star for Ayer Service Flag." A former employee, Thomas O'Bannon, had enlisted in the US Army Air Force in September 1941; he had reported in June that he'd made captain and had won an Air Medal. He was killed on July 24, somewhere in Europe.

Gripping events surrounded the news of Pearl Harbor. In the December 12, 1941, issue, the newsletter reported that "Japan's attack on the United States last Sunday created a number of special problems with regard to advertising for our clients." Bell System's Telephone Hour was prepared. "As early as last September we carefully considered with the client what we should say in the event of war," the newsletter editor wrote. "The Telephone Hour was the first major program on the air after the beginning of hostilities that had been specifically designed to meet the public's need for patriotic inspiration at such a time." Other programs that weren't prepared "either overflowed with patriotic emotion, neglected to mention the war at all, or confused patriotism with advertising in such a way that it offended rather than inspired." The article pointed out that "another well-known national program on Sunday night" ended with the song "This is the end of a perfect day."

The staff assigned to the army account rapidly mobilized. "Less than two hours after the first radio report of the bombing of Pearl Harbor on Sunday, the various members of the organization working on the Army account began planning for a special advertisement," the newsletter reported. They left Philadelphia at 7.00 Monday morning, writing copy and doing layouts on the way to Washington. By 10:00 that morning, more than two hours before President Roosevelt

The N.W. Ayer writers and designers who created this ad found a powerful image for boosting participation in the Fifth War Loan. The war transformed the ads seen by the American public; this one ranks among the most surprising. This ad appeared in New York newspapers in the middle of June 1944. Courtesy, Brooklyn Union Gas Co.

asked Congress to declare war, the ad was submitted and approved by the War Department. It appeared in nearly 1,000 newspapers on December 10.

Other clients also had particular interest in the attack. The newsletter's January 7, 1942, issue noted, "When the quiet of the sunny Sunday San Francisco afternoon of December 7 was suddenly ended by news that the Japs were bombing Pearl Harbor, no food executives in the country had more cause to be excited than did those of the San Francisco office of the Hawaiian Pineapple Company." The Dole cannery was in Honolulu, five miles from Pearl Harbor and two miles from Hickam Field. "The Navy clamped down its censorship. Cables, radio message, telephone conversations were all delayed. Finally, days after the attack, word came that the company's people in the Islands were all safe."

More mundane concerns surfaced as well; many clients had converted to making military material and no longer had commercial products to sell. Caterpillar, "now producing almost exclusively for war purposes,

Bazooka! And the guy turned into a GIANT

This ad, produced by N.W. Ayer for General Electric in late 1943, combined a humorous image with front-line copy. Most other GE ads didn't mention specific military products made by the company. Courtesy, The General Electric Hall of History Foundation

What can you tell an 8-year-old?

ANOTHER REASON TO "DO MORE THAN EVER BEFORE"

Without products to sell, companies maintained their public presence by promoting government-approved campaigns. This pitch for war bonds, produced by N.W. Ayer in 1944, uses an eye-catching image to make the point that things weren't so bad on the homefront during the war. Courtesy, Goodyear Archives

but advertising even more actively than before, is an excellent example of far-sightedness in the maintenance of their contacts through advertising with their normal customer relationships," the newsletter said. In February 1942, an article discussed another sort of non-traditional advertising. "The possibility of substantial increases in the use of telephones because of the defense program was foreseen well in advance, and much of the advertising during 1941 was really in the form of an explanation," asking customers to avoid using the phones at critical times.

By early 1942, the war was affecting Ayer clients in several other ways. A March article described the plight of Atlantic Refining Company. Its supplies had been cut "by arbitrary regulations from Washington," principally of fuel-oil deliveries, and other sorts of rationing were imminent. Delivery schedules were disrupted by

a shortage of tankers, and the remaining ones faced the threat of torpedo attacks in the Gulf.

Wartime worries about security also figured directly into the agency's business. In September 1943, for instance, the army and navy issued directives ordering that no references to radar appear in ads. Ayer already had approval for a General Electric ad mentioning radar, but changed it to conform to the new rules, earning a kudo from a major general from Joint Security Control, who said, "It is in our best judgment that in the interest of the war effort and the men of our armed forces whose lives may depend on Radar, its publicity be played down."

Later issues of the *Ayer News Files* continued to document the trends and events of World War II. Today, those fifty-year-old newsletters depict the war's impact in an unusually diverse and detailed way.

Selected Sources

Books

Advertising and Its Role in War and Peace, Industrial Series No. 5, US Dept. of Commerce, 1943.

America Organizes to Win the War—A Handbook on the American War Effort, Harcourt, Brace and Company, New York, 1942.

"Ayer News File," N.W. Ayer & Son, New York (company newsletter), July–Oct. 1940, Feb.–Dec. 1941, Jan.–April 1942, April–Dec. 1943.

Beaton, Kendall, *Enterprise in Oil—A History of Shell in the United States*, Appleton-Century-Crofts, Incorporated, New York, 1957.

Begley, George, *Keep Mum! Advertising Goes to War*, Lemon Tree Press, London, 1975.

Biederbeck, Thomas (editor), *Caterpillar—Century of Change*, Caterpillar Tractor Company, Peoria, Illinois, 1984.

Campbell, D'Ann, *Women at War with America—Private Lives in a Patriotic Era*, Harvard University Press, 1984.

"Community Silver: A Case Study," *Tide* magazine, June 17, 1949.

Dunham, Terry, and Lawrence Gustin, *The Buick—A Complete History*, Princeton Publishing Company, 1980.

Fox, Stephen, *The Mirror Makers, A History of American Advertising and Its Creators*, Morrow, New York, 1984.

Freedom's Arsenal, The Story of the Automotive Council for War Production, Automobile Manufacturer's Association, Detroit, 1950.

Fussell, Paul, *Wartime—Understanding and Behavior in the Second World War*, Oxford University Press, 1989.

Goodman, Jack (editor), *While You Were Gone, A Report on Wartime Life in America*, Simon and Schuster, New York, 1946.

Hamblin, Dora Jane, *That Was the Life*, W.W. Norton, 1977

Hornung, Clarence, and Fridolf Johnson, *200 Years of American Graphic Art*, George Braziller, Incorporated, New York, 1976.

Kennett, Lee, *For the Duration: The United States Goes to War, Pearl Harbor—1942*, Charles Scribner's Sons, New York, 1985.

Lewine, Harris, *Good-Bye to All That*, McGraw-Hill, 1970.

MacLeish, Archibald, *The American Cause*, Duell, Sloan and Pierce, New York, 1941.

Marchand, Roland, *Advertising the American Dream—Making Way for Modernity, 1920-1940*, University of California Press, 1985.

Mehler, William Jr., *Let the Buyer Have Faith—The Story of Armstrong*, Armstrong World Industries, Incorporated, Lancaster, Pennsylvania, 1987.

Nelson, Donald M., *Arsenal of Democracy*, Harcourt, Brace and Company, New York, 1946.

Nevins, Allan, and Frank Ernest Hill, *Ford: Decline and Rebirth, 1933-1962*, Charles Scribner's Sons, New York, 1963.

Perrett, Geoffrey, *Days of Sadness, Years of Triumph*, Coward, McCann & Geohegan Incorporated, New York, 1973.

Remington, R. Roger, and Barbara J. Hodik, *Nine Pioneers in American Graphic Design*, The MIT Press, Cambridge, Massachusetts, 1989.

Robert, Joseph, *Ethyl—A History of the Corporation and the People Who Made It*, University Press of Virginia, 1983.

Rogers, Donald I., *Since You Went Away*, Arlington House, New York, 1973.

Rupp, Leila, *Mobilizing Women for War: German and American Propaganda 1939-45*, Princeton University Press, 1978.

Seldin, Joseph, *The Golden Fleece*, Macmillan Company, New York, 1963.

Shale, Richard, *Donald Duck Joins Up—The Walt Disney Studio During World War II*, UMI Research Press, Michigan, 1976.

The Stetson Century, 1865-1965, John B. Stetson Company, 1965.

Stout, Wesley, *A War Job "Thought Impossible,"* Chrysler Corporation, Detroit, 1945.

Thruelsen, Richard, *The Grumman Story*, Praeger Publishers, New York, 1976.

Williamson, Harold, *Winchester—The Gun That Won the West*, A. S. Barnes and Company, Incorporated, New York, 1952.

Yenne, Bill, *Rockwell—The Heritage of North American*, Brompton Books Corporation, 1989.

Young, James Webb, *The Diary of an Ad Man—The War Years, June 1, 1942–December 31, 1943*, Advertising Publications, Incorporated, Chicago, 1944.

Zeman, Zbynek, *Selling the War—Art and Propaganda in World War II*, Orbis Publishing Limited, 1978.

Other Sources

Article by Kenneth Davis, advertising specialist, Division of Industrial Economy, in *Domestic Commerce*, May 1943.

Primary source material about the Office of War Information (correspondence, media guides, memoranda, and reports) is from Record Group 208 (Boxes 161, 163, 1126D, 1127, 1138–1140, 1148–1151, and 4063) at the Washington National Records Center in Suitland, Maryland. According to the Introduction to the National Archives OWI files, "During its existence the OWI created approximately 22,500 linear feet of records in the United States." Record Group 208 contains 2,295 linear feet.

Written summary of the OWI-Graphic Arts Victory Committee Conference, March 26, 1943, in Washington, D.C.

Magazines and the War, National Publishers Association, New York; updated pamphlet.

Transcript of remarks by Elmer Davis, director of the OWI, to the New York State Publishers Association, Sept. 14, 1943.

Nelson, Donald, "The High Cost of Victory," article in the *Reader's Digest*, December 1943.

Annual reports from the Association of American Railroads, 1940–1945.

Kelley, Timothy, "A Trip Down Memory Main," *American Gas* magazine, June 1990.

Wartime annual reports of the National Dairy Products Corporation and the General Foods Corporation.

Cheesekraft, employee newsletter of the Kraft Cheese Company, 1942 issues.

The Kraftsman, Kraft Foods, Sept.–Oct. 1973.

Lockheed Horizons, Issue 12, June 1983, "A History of Lockheed," Roy Blay, editor.

Index